P9-DIF-209

The Israel Museum Guide

by Rafi Grafman

The Israel Museum, Jerusalem

Publishing Consultant: Asher Weill
Photographic Editors: Irène Lewitt, Genya Markon
Design: Lakey Teasdale
Plans: Albert Levy

Photographers: David Harris; also Hillel Burger, Ran
Erde, Yoram Lehmann, Reuven Milon, Zeev Rado-
van, Baruch Rimon, Vivienne Silver, Nahum Slapak
Jacket design: Ora Yafeh
Jacket photograph: Leonardo Bezzola

Donors of art objects illustrated in this guide will
be found on pages 171-174
Many of the photographs are published by kind
permission of the Israel Department of Antiquities
and Museums

© The Israel Museum, Jerusalem, 1983
No part of this publication may be reproduced,
stored in a retrieval system or transmitted, in any
form or by any means, electronic, mechanical,
photocopying, recording, or otherwise, without the
prior written permission of the publisher

Printed by Hamakor Press, Jerusalem, 1983

Contents

General Information

Please note:

Visiting hours See p. vii.

The Information Desk is located in the entrance hall of the main building.

The Museum Shop is located in the entrance pavilion and in the entrance hall of the main building.

The Bulletin Board is located behind the information desks, and lists current exhibitions, events and tours.

The Cloak-Room Large bags, knapsacks, umbrellas, cameras and other bulky items should be checked at the cloak-room, located next to the bulletin board.

Rest-rooms For locations, see the plan inside the back cover.

Guided Tours See p. vii.

Museum Services See pp. 168-170.

The Cafeteria is located just off the entrance plaza, opposite the main building entrance, and is open during visiting hours except on Saturdays and Jewish holidays (on Tuesdays only till 8 pm).

No photographing is permitted within the museum galleries. Cameras *must* be checked at the cloakroom.

Please do not touch any of the exhibits — whether objects, paintings or sculpture — unless otherwise labelled. Neither should the cases be touched or leaned upon. Electronic surveillance and alarm systems are in operation in the galleries.

No smoking or eating is permitted within the museum galleries.

No pets or firearms are permitted on the museum grounds.

Wheelchair visitors are most welcome to the Israel Museum, and various installations are provided to facilitate their visit. Wheelchairs are also available on request from the staff. Keys to the special elevators adjacent to most of the stairways within the main building are available from the guard at the main gate. A few galleries in the main building (rooms 104 and 219-221 in the Bezalel section; 316 in archaeology; and 410 in the youth wing), and part of the Shrine of the Book are at present difficult to visit by wheelchair, as is the Library.

Hours of Admission

Main Museum Building: Sunday, Monday, Wednesday, Thursday, 10 am — 5 pm
Tuesday, 4 pm — 10 pm
Friday, Saturday and Jewish holidays, 10 am — 2 pm

Shrine of the Book: Sunday, Monday, Wednesday, Thursday, 10 am — 2 pm
Tuesday, 10 am — 10 pm
Friday, Saturday and Jewish holidays, 10 am — 2 pm

Billy Rose Art Garden: Sunday — Thursday, 10 am — sunset
Friday, Saturday and Jewish holidays, 10 am — 2 pm.

The Israel Museum is *closed* on the Jewish New Year (Rosh Hashanah, two days) and on the eve of Jewish holidays the museum is open until 2 pm. During the summer vacation, check additional visiting times in the daily newspapers.

Guided Tours (free)

Starting at the bulletin board in the entrance hall.

In *English*: Sunday, Monday, Wednesday, Thursday, 11 am
Tuesday, 4:30 pm

In *Hebrew*: Sunday, Monday, Wednesday, 11 am
Tuesday, 4:30 pm

Special Guided Tours (in English, French, German, Spanish and Hebrew), for groups or individuals, should be arranged several days in advance by telephone (02-698211, ext. 213).

Introduction

The Israel Museum, which opened in 1965, is an independent institution which, with the help of all its many friends in Israel and abroad, has been able to develop into a museum of international repute within a short time. Most of its art treasures have been donated by generous benefactors from all over the world.

The Israel Museum integrates five separate entities: the Bezalel National Museum for the fine arts, Judaica and ethnography, (founded in 1906 and named after the biblical craftsman who fashioned the tabernacle for Moses in the wilderness); the Samuel Bronfman Biblical and Archaeological Museum, formed around the collections of the Israel Department of Antiquities and Museums; the unique Billy Rose Sculpture Garden, with sculpture scattered over its five acres of rhythmic walls and terraces; the Ruth Youth Wing; and the Shrine of the Book, the home of the rarest biblical manuscripts in the world. Situated at the crossroads of the past and the present, the museum is flanked by the Monastery of the Cross, the Knesset — Israel's parlia-

ment — and the Hebrew University of Jerusalem. The main building complex of the Israel Museum was designed by the Israeli architectural team of Alfred Mansfeld and Dora Gad. The plan is based on the principle of a fixed module, facilitating standardization and future growth. The image of the complex from afar is that of a Middle Eastern village hugging the hillside, in harmony with the landscape.

The Israel Museum is a thriving center for cultural activities. Nearly one million visitors enter its gates each year, in addition to the 15,000 school-children who utilize its youth wing on a regular basis. Apart from the museum's permanent and temporary exhibitions, there are concert programs, films, numerous special events, lectures and gallery talks. We do hope you enjoy your visit and that you will return again and again.

Martin Weyl
Director

Entering the main gate, and ascending the Carter Walk, past the sculpture *18 Levels* (1971) by the Israeli artist Ya'acov Agam, and then turning to the right, one approaches the Shrine of the Book, the building which houses the Dead Sea Scrolls.

Agam: 18 Levels (1971).

1

Shrine of the Book

The Shrine of the Book, Gottesman Center for Biblical Manuscripts, houses the Dead Sea Scrolls and the Bar Kokhba finds. Its white dome and black wall are symbolic of the struggle between the Sons of Light and the Sons of Darkness, a recurrent theme in the scrolls themselves. The subterranean atmosphere within the building is reminiscent of the caves in which the scrolls were found. The architecture also promotes the stable conditions necessary for the preservation of these precious documents.

The first seven of the Dead Sea Scrolls were discovered in 1947 in a cave near Khirbet Qumran on the northwestern shore of the Dead Sea. Immediately upon their discovery they were recognized as being of revolutionary significance for scholarship, both Jewish and Christian. They were all written on parchment, mostly in Hebrew with a few in Aramaic, and belonged to a Jewish sect, probably the Essenes, who flourished two thousand years ago. The monastery-like buildings of the sect were situated near the caves, overlooking the Dead Sea. Excavations on the site, complemented by the scrolls themselves, have revealed a vivid picture of a communal, ascetic way of life, governed by a deep belief in the final, apocalyptic war between the Sons of Light (the sect) and the Sons of Darkness (the world at large), and in the ultimate coming of the Messiah.

Those of the Dead Sea Scrolls containing the books of the Bible are the oldest known biblical manuscripts, representing every book of the Hebrew Bible but that of Esther. Other of the scrolls contain the religious literature of the Dead Sea sect. This sect was founded sometime in the 2nd century BCE, and was decimated in the great Jewish war against Rome, in 66-73 CE, during which time the Jewish temple in Jerusalem was destroyed.

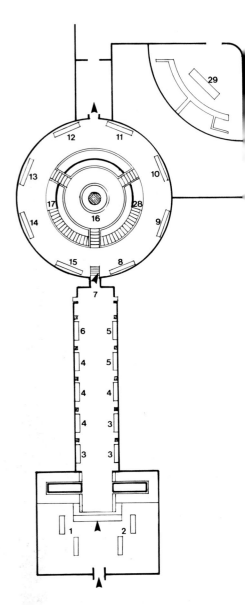

2

A second Jewish revolt against Rome broke out some sixty years later, in 132-135 CE, under the leadership of Shimon Bar Kokhba (or Bar Kosiba). The second major group of manuscripts and objects on display at the Shrine of the Book originates from the period of this later war. In the latter stages of this revolt, some of the Jews of Ein Gedi, on the western shore of the Dead Sea, sought refuge in a cave in Nahal Hever, a nearby canyon cutting through the Judean desert. Here they were besieged by the Roman army and, finally, all perished. Before the end they hid many of their belongings within the cave, including the documents and the fascinatingly well-preserved objects now on display here.

In the *entrance hall*, a series of facsimiles (1) of four ancient manuscripts are compared with a facsimile page of the Aleppo Codex, the oldest surviving manuscript of the complete Hebrew Bible, but only about half as old as the Dead Sea Scrolls. A map of the Dead Sea region (2) shows the sites where the manuscripts in the Shrine of the Book were found, accompanied by photographs of the sites.

The long *passageway* leading to the main hall is reminiscent of the deep, tunnelling cave where the Bar Kokhba letters were found. Until their discovery in 1960-61, the entire Bar Kokhba war was a poorly-documented episode in Jewish history. Today we have fifteen letters (3) from Bar Kokhba himself ("From Shimon son of Kosiba..."), dictated in a pithy, military style and dispatched to his lieutenants at Ein Gedi. They deal with matters of supply, the local populace and discipline. All are written on papyrus, in Hebrew, Aramaic or Greek. Amongst the group of insurgents who had fled to the Cave of Letters in Nahal Hever was

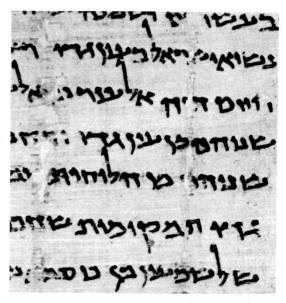

(4) Papyrus document, Bar Kokhba War, 132-135 CE.

a woman named Babata, daughter of one Shimon. The story of this wealthy, twice-married matron is revealed by a bundle of documents found in the cave (4), written in Hebrew, Aramaic, Greek and Nabatean. These texts, including her deed of divorce and other legal papers, provide a unique glance into everyday life on the eastern border of Judea eighteen hundred years ago.

The pottery inkwell (5) was found at Khirbet Qumran, in the room where the scrolls were copied out laboriously by the scribes of the sect.

The waterskin in which the Bar Kokhba Letters were found (6) served as a large pouch; it is made of the entire hide of a sheep, peeled off the carcass in one cylindrical piece.

3

In the *antechamber* to the main hall are two jars (7) made for storing the scrolls. The domed white interior of the *main hall* resembles the shape of the lids of the jars in which the Dead Sea Scrolls were found. On entering, the visitor should turn to the right. Each case can be illuminated by pressing the button in the right-hand corner.

The Manual of Discipline (8) — the code of rules of the Dead Sea sect and its communal life — deals with such matters as new members, conduct at communal meals, punishments, and it concludes with blessings of thanksgiving.

The Scroll of the War of the Sons of Light against the Sons of Darkness (9) is a detailed military manual which outlines the final, apocalyptic conflict. The text lays out the procedure of battle, giving the formations of cavalry and infantry, the types of weapons to be used, the warriors to be recruited, the banners and their holy slogans, and the prayers to be recited; a revealing document on methods of warfare in Roman times.

The *tefillin* (phylacteries; see p. 39) found at Qumran (10) are the earliest known examples of these ritual objects, which observant Jews use to this day in their daily prayers. One set was found in its original leather case, made to hold the four minute parchments, each bearing particular passages from the Torah.

The Habakkuk Commentary (11) is an exposition of the biblical book of Habakkuk. The sectarian commentaries to the various books of the Bible were based on their belief that the Scriptures held hidden references to contemporaneous events relating to the sect, and thus

(7) Scroll jars from Qumran, 1st cent. CE.

they are a prime source for the history of this ancient Jewish faction.

Case (12) is devoted to special, temporary exhibits of ancient manuscripts or related material.

The Psalms Scroll (13) includes forty-one canonical psalms and seven others which have not been included in the canonical Bible. The nature of this scroll, only a part of which is on display, suggests that it was intended for liturgical use.

Only a part of the long *Isaiah Scroll* (14) is on display; a facsimile of the entire scroll can be seen on the central platform (16).

4

Above: (15) The Temple Scroll.   Below: (9) Scroll of the War of the Sons of Light.

A part of the *Temple Scroll* (15), the longest of the Dead Sea Scrolls (almost 9 meters or 30 feet long) is shown here. Over half of the Scroll deals with the temple in Jerusalem, but it also interprets laws concerning kingship, feasts and their sacrifices, and ritual purity.

On the *central platform* (16), in the case resembling the handle of a Torah scroll, is a facsimile of the entire Isaiah Scroll (over 7 meters or 24 feet long), containing all sixty-six chapters of the biblical book. This scroll, copied around 100 BCE, is the oldest complete manuscript of a book of the Bible, and is a thousand years older than any other known complete copy.

Descend the stairway (17) to the *lower central hall*, where we return to the time of the Bar Kokhba war with a selection of objects from the Cave of Letters in the Judean desert. Their condition is so excellent that virtually no restoration work on them was found necessary. On the central column is a plan of the cave (18). The palm-fiber baskets (19) are examples of the many baskets found in the cave which contained many of the other objects on display here: bronze vessels, keys and the like, and the skulls and bones of the refugees.

Opp: The Shrine of the Book.
(24) Iron keys, Bar Kokhba War 132-135 CE.

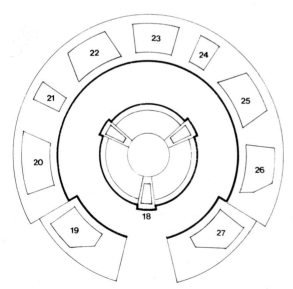

*(26) Roman bronze jug, Bar Kokhba War, 132-135 CE.
Opp: The Billy Rose Sculpture Garden.*

One next sees four bronze incense shovels (20), a libation bowl with handle ("patera") bearing a mythological scene (Thetis riding a sea-monster, bringing armor to her son Achilles at Troy), and a large bowl (note the rope still tied to its handle). These bronze utensils, as well as those in (26), were apparently made in southern Italy and may well have been booty taken from the Roman army during the war. Similar objects have been found at Pompeii in Italy.

Several large iron knives (21) and, below, a "jack-knife" and an arrow, are representative of the tools and weapons found in the cave.

A copper mirror in its wooden case (22), a small basket containing coarse cooking-salt, and several wooden dishes reflect the domestic side of life in the cave.

Of the two fragments of cloth (23), the one on the right was part of a tunic, while that on the left was probably for a scroll.

The several keys (24), both large and small, are of a type which went out of use in the Near East only a century or so ago. They must have locked the homes of those who had fled to the cave from Ein Gedi. The ring-key belonged to a strongbox or jewelry case, and could be worn on the finger for safety.

The large cloth (25) is evidence of the extreme skill of Jewish dyers and weavers in the Roman period. Balls of yarn indicate that women endeavored to continue their normal activities even while hiding in the caves. The bundle of purple unspun wool was intended for the tassels worn at the corners of the *talit* (prayer shawl, see p. 39) by every observant Jew.

More booty taken from the Romans during the Bar Kokhba war are the bronze jugs (26). The human and animal forms on their handles — a winged bust of victory, a mask, a lion's head, a thumb, a paw — have been defaced in keeping with Jewish law against idolatry. One of the jugs, at the lower left, bears a frieze depicting running animals; its handle is rather more elaborate than the others.

The outstanding glass bowl (27) is one of the largest and finest pieces of glass surviving from antiquity; it was found, together with the small glass plate, wrapped in the bundle of palm-frond fibers. The large glass jug was used for keeping oil or wine.

The main hall can be reached again by an ascending stairway (28). From the main hall the exit leads to the bookshop (29), which has on sale postcards, pamphlets, books and slides of the Dead Sea Scrolls, Qum-

(16) Central platform with Isaiah Scroll.

ran, Masada, and the Bar Kokhba caves. (These items may also be purchased at the museum shop.)

Coming back to the Carter Walk and turning right, one again proceeds up the rising, stepped walk towards the main building. Half-way up, on the left, is the entrance to the youth wing. (Though it is possible to go through the youth wing into the main building, it is recommended that your visit begin at its main entrance; moreover, if you are carrying a camera or large bag, you will not be permitted to pass through to the archaeology section from the youth wing).

Continuing on, to the left (2) are two segments of the stone pipeline built in Roman times to bring water to Jerusalem from Solomon's Pools south of Bethlehem. A little beyond (3) is part of a stone door from a Roman-Byzantine tomb; note that it imitates a wooden door complete with iron studs, and in the panels are several "keys" of the very type just seen in the Shrine of the Book.

Further up the walk, opposite the entrance (4) to the *cafeteria*, is (5) Victor Vasarely's *Screen* (1967). To the right is the entrance to the *Billy Rose Sculpture Garden*.

The Billy Rose Sculpture Garden.

Billy Rose Sculpture Garden

Climbing to the top of the *Water Source Sculpture* by Isamu Noguchi, the American sculptor who designed the art garden, there is a view of the entire garden complex. Its high, semicircular terraces, supported by huge retaining walls built of blocks of Jerusalem stone, form a splendid setting for the museum's collection of modern sculpture, the nucleus of which was donated by Billy Rose. Late 19th century and early 20th century sculpture is well represented, including works by Rodin, Bourdelle, Maillol, Archipenko, Zadkine, Nadelman and Freundlich. More recent sculptors include Picasso, Moore, Lipchitz, Epstein, Chadwick, Marini, Tinguely, Arman, Wotruba, Caro and Indiana. Israeli sculptors are represented by David Palombo, Igael Tumarkin, Menashe Kadishman, Michael Gross, Yehiel Shemi, Ezra Orion, Benni Efrat and Yitzhak Danziger.

To visit the Billy Rose and Lipchitz Pavilions, descend from the fountain and, returning past (1), turn right; on the way through the sculpture courtyards are sculptures (2) to (29). Temporary exhibitions of contemporary, often avant garde art, are often held in the Billy Rose Pavilion. The Jacques Lipchitz Pavilion houses 140 bronze sketches donated by Rubin Lipchitz, the sculptor's brother. These pieces, first made in clay, represent the evolution of the artist's ideas from the initial stages of the model. In their directness they express instantaneous ideas: Lipchitz himself called them his "hot cookies". This collection presents the development of a great artist and of modern sculpture as a whole, to which Lipchitz was an important contributor.

The Lipchitz Pavilion also contains a gallery for indoor sculpture from the museum's collections, the display being changed periodically. Here the visitor can see works by Arp, Archipenko, Butterfield, Druks, Duchamp Villon, Marcel Duchamp, Giacometti, Gonzales, Marisol, Nadelman, Nevelson, Pevsner, Stankiewicz, Kienholz, Segal, Trova, Hesse and many other sculptors.

Lipchitz: Bronze Study (1930-31).

(9) Maillol: L'harmonie (1941-42).

Smith: Cubi VI (1963).

13

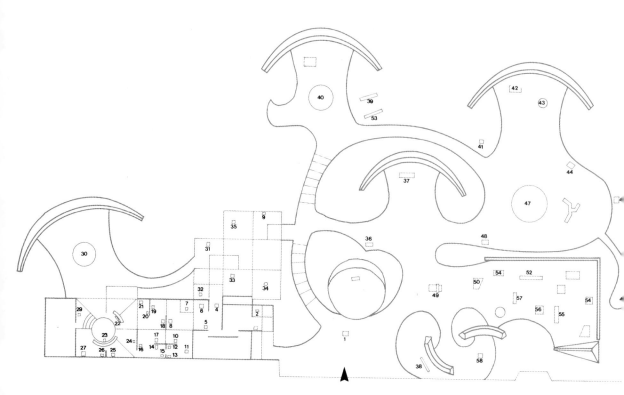

For the visitor walking about the garden, the following list identifies the individual sculptures as numbered in the plan.

1 Marino Marini (Italian), *An Idea in Space*, 1974
2 Elie Nadelman (American), *Man in the Open Air*, ca. 1915
3 José de Creeft (Spanish), *Woman in the Sun*, 1938
4 Otto Freundlich (b. Germany), *Ascension*, 1929
5 Robert Delaunay (French), *Relief*
6 Auguste Rodin (French), *Study for Balzac, Nude*, 1892
7 Germaine Richier (French), *The Diabolo Player*, 1950

8 Ettore Colla (Italian), *Moses*, 1957

9 Aristide Maillol (French), *L'Harmonie*, 1941-42

10 Etienne Hajdu (Rumanian), *Anita*, 1964

11 Chana Orloff (School of Paris), *Pipe Smoker — Portrait of D.O. Widhopff*, 1924

12 Chaim Gross (American), *Mother and Child*, 1956

13 Dina Recanati (Israeli), *Woman*, 1963

14 Jack Zajac (American), *Falling Water VI*, 1967

15 Ivan Mestrovic (Yugoslav), *Moses*, 1926

16 William Zorach (American), *Moses*, 1952

17 Reg Butler (British), *Young Girl with Chemise*, 1957-58

18 Luciano Minguzzi (Italian), *Woman Skipping Rope*, 1954

19 Isamu Noguchi (American), *Khmer*, 1962

20 John Wragg (British), *Beacon*, 1969

21 Robert Adams (British), *Large Screen Form*, 1962

22 Bernard Rosenthal (American), *Oracle*, 1960

23 Jacob Epstein (British), *The Visitation*, 1926

24 Germaine Richier (French), *Torso of a Youth*, ca. 1953

25 Hugo Robus (American), *Annunciation*

26 Koren der Harootian (American) *Rebellious Slave*, 1947

27 Saul Baizerman (American), *Titan*, 1950-57

28 Jacques Lipchitz (School of Paris), *Musical Instruments*, 1918

29 Jacques Lipchitz (School of Paris), *The Bather*, 1917

30 Menashe Kadishman (Israeli), *Suspense*, 1966

31 Auguste Rodin (French), *Adam*, ca. 1880

32 Alexander Archipenko (Russian), *Woman Combing her Hair*, 1914

33 Aristide Maillol (French), *Chained Liberty — Blanqui Monument*, ca. 1906

34 Emile Antoine Bourdelle (French), *La Grande Pénélope*, 1912

35 Ossip Zadkine (School of Paris), *Orpheus*, 1954

36 Emile Antoine Bourdelle (French), *The Warrior of Montauban*, ca. 1898

37 Henry Moore (British), *Vertebrae*, 1968

38 Shlomo Koren (Israeli), *Cylinder in Space*, 1972

39 Igael Tumarkin (Israeli), *Tension*, 1970

40 Yitzhak Danziger (Israeli), *Sheep*, 1960-64

41 Bernard Heiliger (German), *Vertical Motif*, 1967

42 Robert Indiana (American), *Ahava*, 1977

43 Ossip Zadkine (School of Paris), *Prometheus*, 1954

44 Igael Tumarkin (Israeli), *Sculpture*, 1967

45 Jean Tinguely (Swiss), *XK³*, 1965

46 Fritz Wotruba (Austrian), *Falling Woman*, 1944

47 Pablo Picasso (Spanish), *Profile*, 1967

48 Ezra Orion (Israeli), *Sculpture*, 1966

49 Benni Efrat (Israeli), *Extrapolations*, 1978

50 Yehiel Shemi (Israeli), *Mountain Banner*, 1967

51 Arman (French), *Homage to a Garment Section*, 1974

52 David Palombo (Israeli), *Sculpture*, 1966

53 Lynn Chadwick (British), *Roaring Lion*, 1960

54 Sofu Teshigahara (Japanese), *Sculpture*, 1965

55 Wessel Couzijn (Dutch), *Rising Africa*, 1961

56 André Volten (Dutch), *Construction*, 1963-64

57 Henry Moore (British), *Reclining Figure*, 1953-54

58 Jacques Lipchitz (School of Paris), *Mother and Child*, 1941-42

plaza

Anthony Caro (British), *Fairweather Flats*

Michael Gross (Israeli), *Sculpture*, 1969-70

Barbara Hepworth (British), *Square Forms with Circles*, 1963

Buki Schwartz (Israeli), White from 0⁰ to 180⁰, 1969

David Smith (American), Cubi VI, 1964

Victor Vasarely (French), *Screen — 3 pieces*, 1967

Returning to the Ida Crown Plaza, passing (6) Henry Moore's *Relief No. 1* (1959), on the wall of the main building we see, across the plaza to the left, basalt stone fragments (7) of the 2nd-3rd centuries CE, from the synagogue at Khorazin near the Sea of Galilee, as well as an inscribed lintel (8) from the ancient synagogue at Nabratein, also in Galilee. This side of the plaza offers a fine view of the Valley of the Cross, below, and of the Rehavia quarter beyond.

Entering the main building through the glass doors, we find ourselves in the Mayer and Fagen Hall — the main entrance. To the right is the *information desk*. To the left is the *museum shop* (closed on Saturdays and Jewish holidays), where you can purchase museum publications: guides, catalogues, postcards and posters — in addition to books on art and archaeology, museum reproductions and other items and gifts. Foreign currency is accepted, and your purchases can be mailed home, for a modest handling fee. For mail orders from the museum shop, see p. 169.

On the wall beyond the information desk is the *bulletin board*, where you will find information on current exhi-

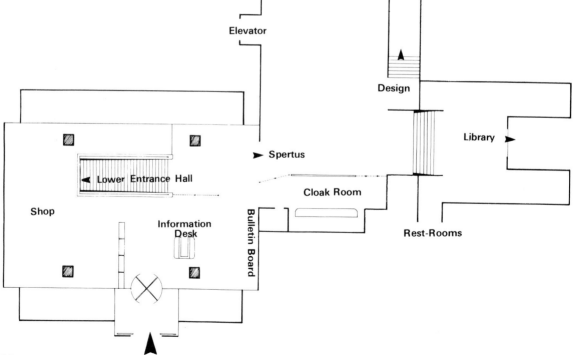

bitions and activities. Free guided tours in English leave from this spot except on Fridays, Saturdays and Jewish holidays: on Sunday, Monday, Wednesday and Thursday, at 11 am; on Tuesday, at 4:30 pm. (For special guided tours, see the bulletin board and p. vii.) The *cloak-room* is located beyond the bulletin board. No photographing is permitted within the galleries; cameras, as well as any bulky items such as large bags, knapsacks and umbrellas, should be checked.

Opposite the cloak-room is the *Spertus Gallery*, which is used for temporary exhibitions. To the right is the *library entrance lobby*, where smaller current exhibitions are shown, often of graphics or photography. The *library* (see p. 168) is entered through the glass doors at the center of the lobby.

Next to the library entrance lobby is the corridor leading to the *Palevsky Design Pavilion*.

Design Pavilion

The prime aim of the design department of the museum and the Palevsky Design Pavilion is to encourage design in Israel by stimulating an awareness of basic precepts and exhibiting the works of international and local designers. Since its inception in 1973, the department has hosted a variety of temporary exhibitions covering a wide spectrum of modern design in such fields as graphics, architecture, industry and social planning.

Major exhibitions have included "Design in Scandinavia" (1974); "Polyhedric Architecture" (Zvi Hecker, Israeli architect, 1976); "Jewelry 1900-1976" (Pforzheim Museum, 1977); "Lego" (1977); "From the End

Product to the Product's End" (Ettore Sottsass, Jr., Italian architect and designer, 1978); "Free Fall, Sheila Hicks at the Israel Museum" (1980); and "Mies van der Rohe: The Barcelona Pavilion and Furniture and Sketches for Furniture" (1980).

The department's small but growing permanent collection includes fine products from Scandinavia, western Europe, the United States, Israel and other lands, and an excellent selection of European posters from the early 1900s to the present. Major architects and designers represented include Charles Rennie Mackintosh, Le Corbusier, Wilhelm Wagenfeld, Marcel Breuer, Charles Eames and Mies van der Rohe.

Returning to the main entrance we descend the stairway to the Goldman-Schwarz Hall. (An elevator is available in the Spertus Gallery.) Here, too, current temporary exhibitions are shown. Turning to the left, you can enter the archaeological section (see p. 86); or, turning back under the stairs, you can enter the numismatic gallery (see p. 83) and reach the museum *auditorium*, or continue on to the ethnic art galleries (see pp. 78-82). In our guidebook tour, however, we shall continue on straight, opposite the stairs, into the galleries exhibiting the collections of Judaica and fine arts.

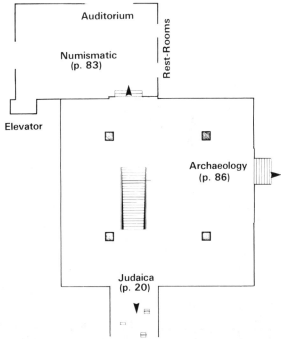

Judaica

One of the outstanding features of the Israel Museum is its collection of Jewish ceremonial art, one of the largest of its kind in the world.

The Jews (anciently called the Hebrews or Israelites) emerged as a people over 3000 years ago in the area today called Israel. Their subsequent history in antiquity is recorded in the Bible. Under David and Solomon, a kingdom was established, with its center in Jerusalem and the temple. After flourishing for over 400 years, this kingdom was destroyed and the Jews were exiled to Babylonia. Less than a century later, however, a new Jewish entity arose in Judea. In the second century BCE it developed into a renewed Jewish state under the Maccabees, and then under Herod and his descendants. During this period, the Bible attained its final form as we know it. Jewish autonomy in antiquity was brought to an end with the Roman capture of Jerusalem and the destruction of the second temple, in 70 CE.

With the dispersion of the Jewish people Judaism ceased to be based solely on the Mosaic laws and the ritual centered around the temple in Jerusalem. Now prayer, study and the oral law — the Mishnah and the Talmud — took on equal significance. The oral law had coalesced out of the day-to-day rulings of the rabbis — the leaders of the numerous Jewish communities mainly in Israel and Babylonia. Slowly the customs and rituals of the Jews set into the forms still practiced, though slight regional differences bear marks, today, of the varying influences of other local cultures. However Jewish prayer has remained standardized and is still based on the order of sacrifices in the temple some 2000 years ago. The seven-branched candlestick which stood in the temple — the *menorah* — became the principal symbol of the Jewish people (1). The stone *menorah* on the right as you enter the Judaica section

is from Hamath-Tiberias on the Sea of Galilee, from the 2nd-3rd centuries CE; the two brass *menorot* on the left demonstrate the continuity of the symbol from antiquity on. They have eight branches and were made in Poland in the 17th-18th centuries (for the Hanukkah festival see p. 31).

Today there are three main Jewish traditions, stemming from the geographical and cultural distribution of the Jews; all three are closely related, differing only in external features. The sefardim or Spanish Jews are the descendants of the Jews of Spain (Hebrew *sefarad*) who were expelled from that land in 1492. They settled especially in North Africa, Italy, the Balkans and Turkey, and have continued to use a Judeo-Spanish dialect ("Ladino", written in Hebrew script) to this day. The oriental Jews are descended from Jews who had settled in various eastern lands in antiquity, and several of their communities have developed very distinctive customs and ways of life, especially in such isolated lands as Yemen. The third major group are the ashkenazim, the Jews of the more northerly parts of Europe (in medieval Hebrew, *ashkenaz* referred to Germany). Their forefathers began moving northward from the Mediterranean basin in medieval times, and came to speak Yiddish (an early German dialect with Hebrew and Slavic, written in Hebrew script).

The Holocaust — the destruction of two-fifths of the Jewish people by the Nazis in 1933-45 — destroyed most of the ashkenazi material culture in Europe; entire communities totally disappeared. This catastrophe subsequently spurred the establishment of the state of Israel in 1948, and the ingathering of Jewish communities from all lands. The Jews in Israel are now in a gradual process of blending into a modern, unified Jewish community, and the revitalized Hebrew language is an outstanding factor in facilitating this.

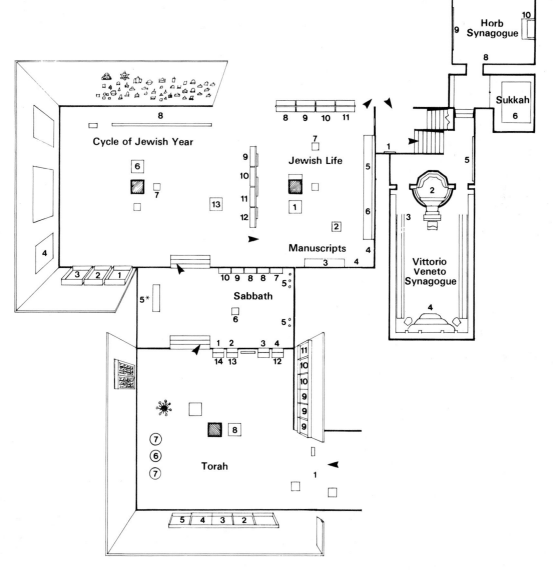

Horb
Synagogue
9   10

8

Sukkah
6

Cycle of Jewish Year

8

6

7

13

8 9 10 11

Jewish Life
7

9

10

11

12

1

2

1

5

6

4

3   4

Manuscripts

1

5

2

3

Vittorio
Veneto
Synagogue

4

Sabbath
10 9 8 8 7 5

5*

6

5

1 2   3 4

11

14 13   12

10

10

9

9

9

8

7

6

7

Torah

1

5 4 3 2

23

The Torah and its Ornaments

(3) Ivory Torah pointer, Central Europe, 18th cent.

The basis of the Jewish religion lies in the Torah — the Pentateuch or first five books of the Bible — the theme depicted in the Fain Gallery. The Torah as read in the synagogue is always in scroll form (2, 3). These scrolls are adorned with various ornaments, mostly named after ancient Israelite ritual objects. Amongst the ashkenazim and some sefardim, the outer cover of the Torah scroll is the *me'il* (mantle) (2, No. 2; 3, No. 3), which is often richly embroidered. Above the scroll's rods and handles (*atzei hayim*, trees-of-life) are the finials, called *rimonim* (pomegranates) (2, No. 1; 3, No. 1). Along with or instead of these *rimonim* there is often a *keter* or *atarah* (crown) (3, No. 3). The *yad* (hand) is the pointer used in reading from the Torah scroll, to avoid touching the sacred parchment or leather (2, Nos. 6-10; 3, Nos. 6-10). The scrolls are kept in an *aron kodesh* or *heikhal* (ark of the law), which is usually draped with a *parokhet* (curtain) (4). An *avnet* (cloth binder; German *Wimpel*) is often tied around the closed scroll (5). Amongst some German and Italian Jewish communities the swaddling cloth used during an infant's circumcision ceremony (see p. 39) was cut and resewn to form a long strip which was presented to the synagogue upon the child's first visit there, or at his bar mitzvah (confirmation at the age of thirteen; see p. 39), to be used as a Torah binder. These were often embroidered or painted with an inscription including the child's name (5, No. 5), birthdate and a blessing, accompanied by various motifs such as a sign of the zodiac (5, Nos. 1-3), the Torah and its ark (referring to the bar mitzvah; 5, No. 2) and a bridal couple beneath a canopy.

Suspended on the front of the Torah scroll, over the *me'il*, is the *tas* (plaque or breastplate) (6). Amongst the oriental communities and most sefardim, the outer cover of the Torah scroll is in the form of a cylindrical box called a *tiq* (case), often richly adorned (7). The two examples of oriental Torah cases are from Persia and the Iraqi community in India; case (6) shows a German Torah; and case (8), an Italian Torah in full regalia.

These Torah ornaments vary from community to community, as does their style. Many of them, especially those from Europe, were made by non-Jewish artisans to Jewish order, though in oriental lands they were usually made by Jewish craftsmen. Such articles were donated to a synagogue, and many of them bear dedicatory or memorial inscriptions, usually in Hebrew, often containing names and dates.

In case (9) are several breastplates depicting Moses and Aaron, the high priest. Weekly portions of the Torah are read in the synagogue in a yearly cycle beginning and ending in the autumn (the festival of *Sukkot* or Tabernacles; see p. 30); in case (10) are breastplates with plaques bearing the names of festi-

vals (*Shavuot*, Pentecost; *Pesach*, Passover, and the like), used in marking the scrolls to be read from on these occasions. Case (11) contains a rare breastplate from Turkey, of circular form.

Case (12) includes a splendid pair of Italian *rimonim* of the 17th century, and a fine Polish crown from 1915. In case (13), the German crown above, from 1793, bears the symbol of the Jewish priests — a pair of hands with fingers spread out in pairs. An unusual Turkish crown with *rimonim* is seen below. Case (14) contains a small pair of enameled *rimonim* from Afghanistan (No. 3), and a pair of gilt *rimonim* made in Jerusalem in 1925. In case (15), No. 3 is a single Persian *rimon* of exceptional beauty; No. 5 is a simple pair of brass *rimonim* from Yemen; No. 6, below, was made of wood in Tunisia; and there are several elegant *rimonim* from Morocco as well.

Throughout Europe, many synagogues were illuminated by elaborate chandeliers such as the pewter candelabrum shown here (16), made in eastern Europe in the 18th century.

The wooden doors (17) and the inscribed lintel above, of the 11th and 13th centuries, are from the Ibn Ezra Synagogue in Old Cairo. The carving is in the fine Fatimid style of Islamic art. Maimonides, the medieval philosopher, may have prayed in this synagogue.

(7) Torah case, Persia, 1799.

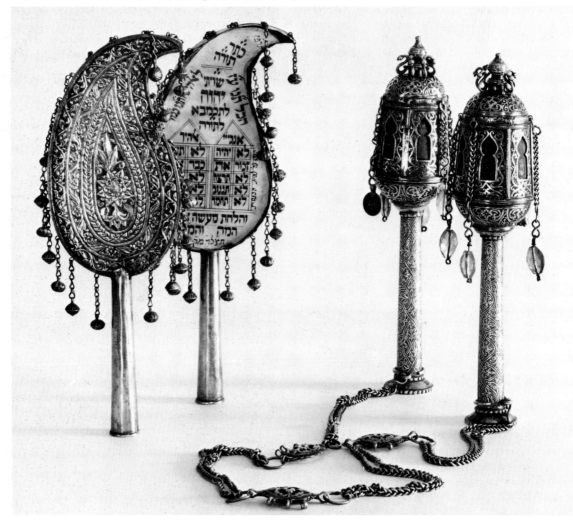

(15) Torah finials: left, Persia, 20th cent.; right, Morocco, 19th cent.

The Sabbath

The Jewish Sabbath, celebrated from sundown on Friday till after dusk on Saturday, is the subject of the Ellern Gallery. The Sabbath is regarded as a festival in its own right, with its own significance, customs, foods, clothing and utensils. Traditionally, many hours are spent on this day in prayer and study. The Friday evening meal is preceded by the *kiddush* (sanctification) blessing, made over a cup of wine. The cup itself, in goblet or beaker form, is often made of a precious metal. In case (1), Nos. 3 and 4 (Russian, 19th century, and German, 1761) are typical ashkenazi goblets; in case (2), No. 2 is a fine 19th century Moroccan beaker, and No. 7, a typical Bokharan *kiddush* goblet of the 19th century. Often the wine-bottles were ornamented as well, as is one example in amber glass, from Syria, bearing part of the blessings (2, No. 4).

Just before sundown on Friday, the housewife kindles the special Sabbath lights and recites a blessing. The 18th century Polish candlestick (2, No. 8) is a very typical ashkenazi form. Early European Sabbath lamps were of the hanging type with a star-shaped oil-container (3, No. 1), which came to be called the *Judenstern* (Jews' star) in German. In North Africa, an oil-lamp with two or four wicks was lit (3, No. 2).

Most articles specifically made for use on the Sabbath — such as silver prayer-book covers (4) — are particularly ornate and are often inscribed in Hebrew; No. 1 is a rare, delicately decorated 16th century Italian filigree and niello-work cover.

Of the group of five hanging *Judenstern* lamps (5), No. 2 is a fine piece of English silversmithing, dated 1813. On Saturday eve, just after dark, the ceremony of *havdalah* marks the transition from the holy Sabbath to the profane days of the week. In this ritual, performed in the home, the blessings of thanks for the past Sabbath are made over wine, spices and light Oriental and

(2) Sabbath wine bottle, Syria, 18th-19th cents.

(2) Kiddush cup, Morocco, 19th cent.

sefardi Jews use a myrtle branch to represent the spices, while the ashkenazim use various dried spices, placing them in a special container, called a *hadas* (myrtle), often in the form of a medieval tower. In case (6) we see an ornate tower for spices, made in Augsburg, Germany, around 1700. Note the figure on the stem, and armed guards at the corners. The adjacent

candle-holder, made in Frankfurt, Germany, in 1741, also has a figure on the stem, holding a beaker and a spice-box; on the corners are four bearded figures. Note the special, braided candle used for *havdalah*. The gold beaker, also from Frankfurt, bears an inscription dated 1765; the biblical scenes in the panels are of Jacob's dream and the sacrifice of Isaac.

28

(10) Spicebox, Moravia, early 19th cent.,

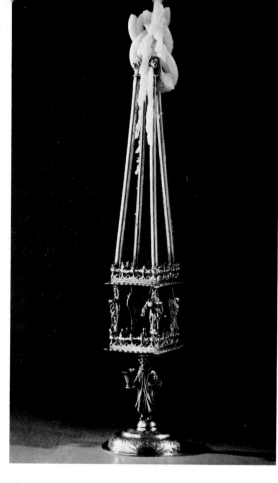

(6) Havdalah candleholder, Germany, early 18th cent.

The spice-towers were often surmounted by ornate flags, as in case (7), Nos. 5-8 and (8), Nos. 7-9. From the 18th century on, various other forms of spice-boxes appear, including a balloon (8, No. 3) a locomotive (8, No. 4), a bird (8, No. 5), flowers and fruits (9, Nos. 1-4), and fish (9, Nos. 5-7). Cases (9) and (10) contain additional spice-towers made in silver; (9), Nos. 10-11 with elaborate flags; and (10), Nos. 8-9, from 18th century Germany, the former with many small gilt figures, and the latter with four figures in the corners, holding a cup of wine, a *havdalah* candle, a prayer-book and a spice-box resembling that in case (8), No. 6. Case (10), above, contains Near Eastern and North African spice and rose water containers used for *havdalah*.

The Cycle of the Jewish Year

(2) Shofar (ram's horn), Germany, 18th cent.

The Jewish year, shown in the Petrie Gallery, begins with the New Year *(Rosh Hashanah)*, which according to the Hebrew calendar, falls in autumn (September-October). It is customary to wear white garments and other special attire (1, Nos. 5-6) for this festival, as well as for the Day of Atonement *(Yom Kippur)*, which, together, are known as the high holidays. Between the two holy days, eight days apart, special early morning prayers are offered, and the synagogue beadle woke the worshippers by knocking on the shutters with a hammer (1, bottom). On both holidays, the *shofar* (ram's horn) is sounded at the synagogue; two of these horns (2, right, from Hungary and Germany) are inscribed and ornamented, while the others here, used especially by oriental Jews, are naturally spiraled or gracefully curved. The Day of Atonement is the most solemn of all Jewish holidays and is devoted to prayer, fasting and penitence.

The week-long *Sukkot* festival — the Feast of Tabernacles or Booths — starts five days after the Day of Atonement, and commemorates the wanderings of the Israelites after the Exodus from Egypt. This festival is celebrated in a *sukkah*, a temporary booth in which all meals are taken during the week of the festival. The *sukkah* is festooned with leaves, flowers and fruits, and it has a roof of branches through which one is able to see the sky. The festival is also symbolized by four plants: the *lulav* (palm frond), *hadas* (myrtle), *aravah* (willow branch); and the *etrog* (citron fruit). The first three plants are usually bound together, and all four are blessed in commemoration of their use in the temple ritual. Along with the *shofar* and the *menorah*, they often appear in ancient Jewish art as major Jewish symbols (see p. 139). The *etrog* is traditionally kept in a special container, particularly amongst the ashkenazim. These boxes assume many forms and are made of many different materials — (3): No. 1, a coconut; No. 3, beads; No. 4, cloves; No. 6, cobalt glass; No. 8, a brass basket; and No. 10, a bird in silver, from the Near East. The 17th century Dutch painter Emanuel de Witte (4) depicted the interior of the Portuguese synagogue in Amsterdam (still standing) shortly after its construction. Note the hanging lamps, reminiscent of (16) in room 201 (p. 25).

Amulets have been popular amongst the Jews since antiquity, and they are found in use amongst all the communities. They were intended to protect the bearer and his possessions from evil and disease, to heal, promote fertility, bring success or evoke love. Case (5*) shows a brief selection. They are made of diverse materials, in many different techniques, and in many of them the material is an integral magical element. A large number bear Hebrew inscriptions, often mystical in nature, invoking divine assistance or appealing to various angels. The *hamsa* hand form (right-hand group, Nos. 9-11) was especially popular amongst Jews in Muslim lands.

The *mezuzah* (doorpost scroll) is affixed to the door posts in a Jewish house in accordance with a commandment in the Torah. The minute scroll includes the biblical passages (Deuteronomy 6:4-9; 11:13-21) beginning "Hear, O Israel, the Lord our God, the Lord is one." The *mezuzah* cases take many forms and use varied materials — porcelain (No. 2, from Germany), wood (No. 4, from Germany), metal (No. 7, made at the Bezalel School of Art in Jerusalem, in the 1920s), and embroidered cloth (No. 8, from Morocco).

The eight-day *Hanukkah* (dedication) holiday (or Festival of Lights) commemorates the reconsecration of the temple in Jerusalem by the Maccabees in 165 BCE, after it had been defiled by the Syrians. During this

Above right: (8) Yemenite lamp, Jerusalem, 20th cent.
Below right: (8) Hanukkah lamp, Germany, 18th cent.
Below left: (8) Hanukkah lamp, France or Spain, 14th cent.

home festival, the lights blessed are held in a special lamp *(hanukkiyah,* in modern Hebrew), which has a row of eight oil containers or candle-holders, with a ninth one, the *shamash* or servitor, separated from the others. One light is lit with the *shamash* on the first night, and on every subsequent night an additional light is kindled, till all eight and the *shamash* are ablaze. The earliest extant examples of such lamps, from 14th century southern France or northern Spain (as well as many subsequent types), are of architectural form. In later periods they took on other forms, such as the "bench" type made of glass beads in Jerusalem, or of pottery from Germany and the Ukraine. The set of nine silver cups for oil, at the bottom, is from Afghanistan.

The three cases arranged around the central pillar (7) contain a selection of unique *hanukkiyot* from the museum collections, which are changed from time to time. One of the three is usually of the standing, nine-branched type *(menorah),* common in Europe from the 18th century on.

On the wall (8) is a wide selection of *hanukkiyot* from many lands, made in various materials and styles. Note especially (from right to left): No. 2, the austere brass lamp from 18th century Holland; No. 6, the ornate filigree type from 19th century Ukraine; No. 7, in the form of an 18th century Polish synagogue; No. 13, from southern Germany, made in pewter around 1780; No. 12, the mirrored lamp from 19th century Germany, No. 16, a handsome 19th century brass lamp from Morocco; No. 31, with its hand-shaped amulets, from Iraq; Nos. 19-22, 24 and 26-30, the group of exquisite Italian lamps from the period of the Renaissance onward; No. 23, from southern France or northern Spain, of the 14th century — one of the earliest known *hanukkiyot*; No. 33, from Salonika in Greece; Nos. 34-41, brass lamps from North Africa; Nos. 42-44, brass lamps made in Jerusalem during the 19th century; No. 45, the Star of David typical of the *hanukkiyot* of India; and Nos. 47-54, stone and pottery lamps from Yemen and North Africa.

Crossing the hall to case (9), we arrive at the *Purim* (drawing of lots) festival, celebrated toward the spring, in commemoration of the salvation of the Jews in the Persian empire, as recorded in the biblical *Megillat Esther* (Scroll of Esther). This is a popular holiday, with much merry-making, even in the synagogue. The 18th century German pewter plates (Nos. 1-2) were used for bringing traditional gifts of cakes and other foods to friends. The silver noisemakers (Nos. 4-6 were wielded by children in the synagogue, during the reading of the *Megillah*, to drown out the mention of the villain Haman's name. Members of the congregation would often follow the reading of the story in elaborately ornamented and encased scrolls (Nos. 8-9; see p. 32).

The week long *Pesach* (Passover) holiday — the main spring festival — is a very ancient festival, richest of all in tradition, commemorating the exodus of the Israelites from Egypt, under the leadership of Moses, some 3300 years ago. On the first night the *Hagaddah* (recitation) is read (10, No. 5; see p. 37) at home, during which the festive meal is partaken. This ceremony, the *seder* (order), includes blessings, prayers, hymns and stories concerning the exodus and the holiday itself. The instructive nature of the *Hagaddah* is clearly revealed by the passage: "And thou shalt tell thy son... 'It is because of that which the Lord did for me when I came forth from Egypt'" — for each Jew is to regard himself as having taken part in the Exodus.

(10) Passover haroset dish, Poland, 18th-19th cents.

During the reading of the *Hagaddah*, in most Jewish communities, the head of the household has before him on the table a large plate with the symbolic foods of the festival. The 18th century pewter *seder* plate (10, No. 6) shows a goat at the center, possibly representing the paschal lamb, and around the rim are illustrations to a popular song sung at the end of the *seder* (*Had Gadya*, One Kid). The large, colorful faience plate (11, No. 4), from 17th century Italy, was painted by a Jewish artist, and bears scenes of the *Pesach* meal, as well as biblical scenes such as the sacrifice of Isaac, and biblical figures (Moses, Aaron, David and Solomon), with the *Pesach* blessings inscribed in Hebrew in the center.

Principal of the symbolic *Pesach* foods is the *matzah* (unleavened bread), the "bread of affliction", unleavened because the Israelites, in their haste to leave Egypt, did not have time to wait for the dough to rise. Often the ritual three pieces of *matzot* are placed in a special, embroidered cover such as (10), No. 7, bearing a blessing and various *Pesach* symbols. The other symbolic foods are *karpas* (a green vegetable), token of the

(13) Passover seder plate, Spain, 15th cent.

Israelites (Exodus 6:6-7). A special fifth cup of wine, symbolic of a further promise to bring the Israelites into the promised land, is traditionally reserved for the prophet Elijah who, it is hoped, will come on *Pesach* and hail the appearance of the Messiah. In case (10), No. 4 is a silver cup of Elijah from 18th century Germany, while Nos. 8 and 9 are of 19th century Bohemian glass.

In case (12) are several calendars for reckoning the days of the *Omer* (sheaf), the 49 days between the first day of *Pesach* and the first day of *Shavuot*, the Festival of Weeks (Pentecost). *Shavuot* occurs at harvest time and was one of the three Jewish festivals of pilgrimage to Jerusalem in antiquity. Traditionally it is also considered the day on which God gave the Torah to the Israelites on Mount Sinai.

Case (13) contains a large seder plate in the Hispano-Moresque style, typical of Spain in the second half of the 15th century. This is one of the very few objects surviving from the Jewish community which existed in Spain prior to the expulsion of the Jews in 1492. (The inscription denoting the main ritual *seder* foods contains several Hebrew spelling errors.)

produce of the earth; *maror* (a bitter herb), symbolic of the affliction of the Israelites in Egypt; *haroset* (a mixture of ground nuts, fruits, spices and wine), symbolic of the mortar used by the Israelite slaves in Egypt (10, No. 10 is a silver wheelbarrow from 19th century Poland, made to hold the *haroset* mixture); *zroa* (limb, a roasted shankbone), representing the paschal sacrifice; and *betzah* (egg), symbolic of a sacrifice brought to the temple in antiquity. Often special plates were made for the *seder*, with places marked for each of the individual foods (11, bottom). During the reading of the *Hagaddah*, each person at the *seder* blesses and drinks four cups of wine (10, No. 3 — a German wine goblet from the 18th century). The four cups are symbolic of the four divine promises of redemption made to the

Continuing to the panels (14), we come to a folk-art which was common throughout Europe in recent centuries — the paper cut-out. This art was adapted for Jewish purposes in the form of decorations for the *sukkah* (see p. 41), calendars for the reckoning of the *Omer* (see above), and ornamental plaques marking the direction of prayer toward Jerusalem, usually eastwards. The latter ornaments are called *mizrah* (east), which popularly is regarded as a Hebrew acronym for "From this flank is the spirit of life." *Mizrahs* were often made and presented as wedding gifts.

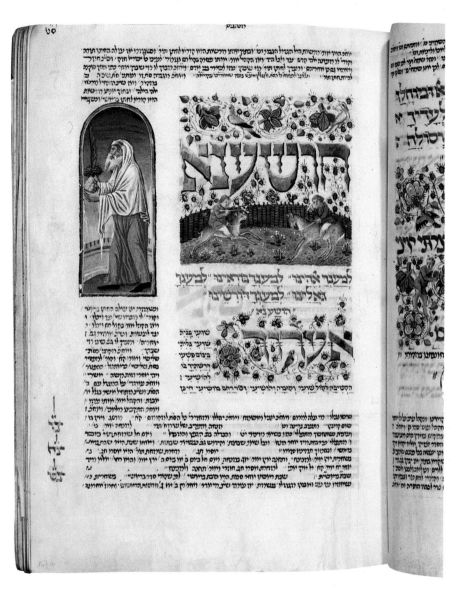

Page from the Rothschild Miscellany, Italy, 15th cent.

Jewish Manuscripts

(3) Birds' Head Haggadah (detail), Germany, ca. 1300.
Opp: Attire of Jewish bride, San'a, Yemen, 19th-20th cents.

The world of Jewish manuscripts is introduced in the Bentinck Gallery by the De Castro pentateuch in case (1), copied in Germany in 1344. This huge parchment tome contains the five books of the Torah and the five *megillot* (Song of Songs, book of Ruth, Lamentations, Ecclesiastes and scroll of Esther) with an Aramaic translation (Onkelos), the fullest Rashi commentary known, the *masorah* (scribal notations) and a colophon giving the names of the scribe and his patron, as well as the date. Fourteen pages are illuminated.

Another unique manuscript is the Rothschild Miscellany (2), a 949-page work written and illuminated in full color on parchment in northern Italy around 1470. It contains over fifty separate religious and secular works (including the Passover *Hagaddah*). The beauty and importance of this manuscript, the illumination of which must have taken several years, lie in the variety and quality of the paintings, which appear on almost every page and depict many facets of Jewish life in the 15th century.

Case (3) contains several manuscript *Hagaddot* from the museum's collections, including the Bird's Head *Hagaddah* from the upper Rhineland in Germany, written around 1300, in which all the Jewish figures are depicted with birds' heads, apparently in compliance with the biblical prohibition of graven images (note the typical medieval Jewish hats) and the Yahudah *Hagaddah*, written in the mid 15th century in southern Germany and containing numerous late medieval depictions. Other manuscripts are occasionally displayed here as well, on a rotational basis.

On the wall above (4), and to the left, are various *ketubot* — Jewish marriage contracts from the museum's collections. Amongst several communities — mainly in Yemen, Persia, Syria and Israel, and especially in Italy — such contracts were not mere written

(3) Yahudah Haggadah, Southern Germany, 15th cent.

documents but became works of splendid ornamentation. In the Near East this usually took on a carpet form, while in Italy contemporaneous 18th and 19th century ornamental styles are seen, with biblical motifs interspersed.

The long wall case (5) contains a *Megillat Esther*, the ornamental frames of which were engraved by Salom Italia, an Italian Jewish artist working in Holland in 1640. The long case beneath (6) displays various *megillot* and their cases.

Jewish Life

In the Flacks gallery we see a case (7) with a small silver casket made in Italy in the 15th century. The lid bears eight dials allowing the owner to record types and quantities of household linens, while on the front is a three-part scene showing the basic duties of a Jewish housewife (left to right): kindling the Sabbath lights, ritual bathing and setting aside a part of the *hallah* (Sabbath bread) dough as a symbolic offering. The theme here indicates that the box was a bridal gift. All the inscriptions on the box are in Hebrew script. The ornamentation is in the niello (black inlay) technique, and the entire casket is a unique piece of fine workmanship.

(7) Jewish bride's box, Northern Italy, 15th cent.

Cases (8-11) outline the Jewish cycle of life, from birth to death. In case (8) we see the knives and clamps used in the *Brit Milah* — the circumcision ceremony which initiates the Jewish male infant into the covenant (Hebrew: *brit*) of Abraham. The cups were used for giving the infant some wine and for receiving the foreskin, while the small flasks were for disinfectant powder. The *mohel* (circumciser) would often record the circumcisions he performed in a special notebook, and such records are often valuable historical documents. Just as the instruments were mostly of precious metals, special clothing was often made for the infant to wear during this ceremony (9, left — both cape and cap are from 19th-century Germany). In most Jewish communities an amulet was tied to the infant to protect him; the example shown here (9, lower right) is from 19th-century Germany.

A Jewish woman's first male issue — like any other "first fruit" — was dedicated to the temple in Jerusalem, and thus had to be "redeemed" from the priests; special tokens and coins were made (and still are) for

the *Pidyon Haben* (redemption of the son) ceremony and, in certain communities, silver vessels were given "in payment" instead (9, lower middle — a 19th-century plate from Galicia, depicting the sacrifice of Isaac).

At the age of thirteen, the Jewish male assumes the responsibilities of manhood, and from then on he must uphold the religious precepts (Hebrew: *mitzvot*). It has long been the custom for the youth to partake actively for the first time in the reading of the Torah at the synagogue on this occasion. He also begins to don daily the *tefillin* (phylacteries) — leather straps and cases containing minute scrolls with biblical texts (see p. 4), in accord with biblical law. At this time, too, his parents present him with a *talit* (prayer-shawl), which he wears for prayer. Often he receives a special bag, usually embroidered, to keep the *talit* and *tefillin* (9, upper right, from Morocco), and in Central Europe it was a custom to protect the leather *tefillin* boxes in special silver cases (9, on the shelf; adjacent is a wooden form for making *tefillin* boxes).

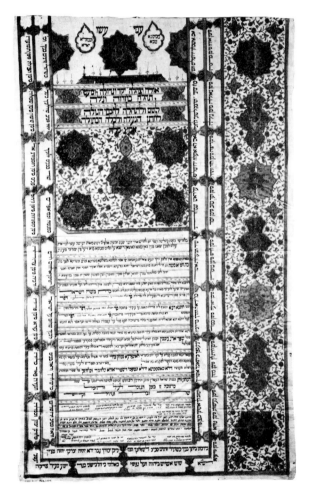

(10) Ketubah (marriage contract), Persia, 19th cent.

Case (10) displays objects associated with the Jewish wedding. We have already seen ornamented *ketubot* (marriage contracts), across the hall (see above); the Italian one shown here (on the back panel), from 1768, is more austere. At the top, as on many *ketubot*, is the passage: "The voice of joy and the voice of gladness". According to Jewish law, a marriage is considered binding only if the groom has given his bride some object of value (be it merely nominal). From medieval times it has been the custom to give a ring and in certain communities such rings have assumed rather ornate forms. The rings shown here (10, on the shelf) are gold filigree work, apparently from 17th century Italy, and were used at the wedding ceremony. The miniature houses mounted on some of them are symbolic of the household being established by the marriage. In Germany special bridal belts often exchanged between groom and bride were occasionally even linked together (10, bottom). During the 19th century in Germany and in Holland, special commemorative medals were sometimes struck to commemorate a wedding (see p. 83).

Charity was most often the concern of various benevolent societies *(hevrot kadisha)* within the Jewish community, and their alms boxes (11, left on the shelf, and bottom) were often elaborate. The dominant societies have always been those concerned with death and burial. These were organized in a manner reminiscent of the trade guilds of Europe, with elected officers, annual banquets and special utensils and vessels, such as the huge glass beaker from Prague (11, upper right) dated 1713 and depicting a burial procession with women mourners following and an alms collector at the end. The adjacent silver comb and a set of small instruments were used in burial preparations.

The Synagogue

Passing into room 208 and turning sharply to the right, one enters the realm of the synagogue, the Jewish house of prayer. The heart of a synagogue is its ark, which contains the Torah scrolls; and the *tevah* or *bemah* (lectern or platform) where the weekly portion of the Torah is read.

The synagogue from Vittorio Veneto in northern Italy, built in baroque style in 1701, went out of use at the end of the First World War and its interior was dismantled and brought to the Israel Museum in 1964 through the generosity of Jakob Michael, in memory of his wife, Erna Michael. In the upper foyer (1) is a small fountain for washing the hands prior to prayer (note the two incised angels, outlined in white). By descending the stairs and turning to the right, one enters the synagogue, alongside the wood-panelled *bemah* (2). Immediately before the *bemah* is a chair of Elijah (3), not from Vittorio Veneto; this late 17th century chair, inscribed in Hebrew with the words "They shall make a covenant", was used in the circumcision ceremony (see p. 39). Opposite is the richly gilded ark of the law (4), inscribed in Hebrew at the top with the words: "Know before whom you stand...." Above it are lattices concealing the women's gallery; in most synagogues the women are segregated from the male worshippers in the main hall, so as not to distract them from their devotions.

Returning to the foyer, on the right is case (5) containing various Italian Torah ornaments of the 17th-19th centuries; No. 3 is a pair of early 18th century *rimonim* from Vittorio Veneto. Continuing into the world of southern German Jewry, we encounter a painted *sukkah* ("booth" or "tabernacle") of the early 19th century (6), from the small village of Fischach in Swabia. On the festival of *Sukkot* (see p. 30) all meals are served in such temporary, symbolic "dwellings". The *sukkah* before us depicts the city of Jerusalem in a colorful, naive style, with the Western Wall of the temple mount at the center.

Opposite the *sukkah*, in case (7), is a splendid *talit* from 18th century Venice (No. 1), and a small *talit* or *arba kanfot* — the small fringed under-shawl worn by observant male Jews (No. 3; hand-woven and embroidered in Syria or Turkey in the 19th century). Beyond the *sukkah* we enter the interior of a small village synagogue (8) from Horb, near Bamberg in southern Germany. The entire wood-panelled vault was painted in 1735 by Eliezer Susmann, who decorated other similar synagogues in the same region, most of which were later destroyed by the Nazis. The style, with its flowing branches interspersed with real and imaginary animals, derives from the painted synagogues of Poland, the land of Susmann's origins. The painted Ark of the Law (9) is located directly opposite a painted and gilt double chair of Elijah (10) from the mid 18th century, used for the circumcision ceremony; it is not originally from this synagogue.

Returning up the stairs and re-entering room 208, we proceed to the display of Jewish ethnography.

Jewish Ethnography

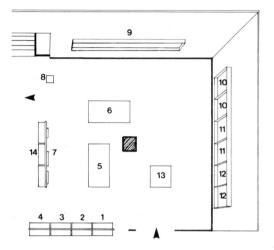

(1) Belt buckle, Ottoman Empire, late 19th cent.

From its earliest days, the museum has pursued the systematic collection of ethnographic objects from the various Jewish communities now living in Israel, concentrating on the Yemenite, Bokharan, Kurdish, Turkish, Afghan, Moroccan and, lately, ashkenazi communities. Priorities in such fieldwork are often determined by the fact that the authentic material culture of many Jewish communities is rapidly disappearing. The Julia and Leo Forchheimer Department for Jewish Ethnography seeks to reconstruct a picture of Jewish life in various lands, displaying the results of its research in a series of exhibitions. Focus is upon the daily life and crafts of the communities, seeking out what is specifically Jewish. Thus, the ethnography collections and the Judaica collections — the latter mainly concerned with ritual objects and the religious aspects of Jewish life — complement one another.

At present the ethnography collection encompasses about 10,000 items, ranging from formal costumes, gold jewelry and heavily embroidered tapestries to the simplest household and craft implements. Two outstanding ethnographic collections have been obtained for the museum: the Salman Schocken Collection of Yemenite objects (on extended loan), gathered in Yemen in the 1920s and 1930s by Carl Rathjens of Hamburg; and the Z. Schulmann Collection, gathered by the collector in North Africa, especially Morocco, in the 1950s.

In the permanent exhibition of Jewish ethnography in room 208, presenting highlights from the department's collection, six ethnic groups are represented: Turkish, Yemenite, Bokharan, North African, Kurdish and Eastern European (ashkenazi).

In case (1) are typical Turkish embroideries, some with gold thread, and a pair of tall wooden clogs inlaid with mother-of-pearl and embroidered, all part of a Jewish bride's dowry. Case (2) shows the fascinating Bokharan variant of tie-dyed silks, colorfully embroidered women's boots, and a sample of gold head ornaments. Cases (3-4) are devoted to Yemen: case (3) shows

Yemenite rural embroidery and jewelry, which is less refined than their counterparts from San'a, the capital of Yemen, seen in case (4). Of special interest is the use of metallic elements in the embroidery, and the intricate patterns on the woman's leggings, at the bottom of case (4).

In the large case (5) are a Bokharan man's coat embroidered in gold thread on velvet and a woman's brocade robe. Below are various embroidered caps and belts. The adjacent case (6) contains two magnificent women's dresses from Spanish Morocco, made of velvet with heavy gold embroidery.

On panel (7), opposite, are three paintings depicting Jewish women's costumes (from left to right): Balkan, mid 19th century; Moroccan, 19th century — *Jewish Woman and Negress*, by Alfred Dehodencq (1822-1882); and Polish — by Isidor Kaufmann (1853-1921). In the small case (8) is an elegant Bokharan gold headpiece, with pearl and tourmaline pendants descending to the eyes. In the long wall case (9) are groups of jewelry from several lands (from left to right): fine silver-gilt filigree work from Yemen; Iranian gold filigree, gems and painted enamel; Bokharan filigree and bold gold work with stones and pearls; and the heavy, variegated North African work, strong in character, some with crude enamel or studded with stones.

In the large wall case (10-12) are groups of Jewish costumes and ornaments from North Africa: Tunisia (10); the delicate work of Algeria (11; note the tall filigree head-dress); and the heavier work from the Atlas mountains of Morocco (12; the massiveness of the ornaments here is a common feature amongst mountain peoples everywhere). A typical feature of jewelry throughout North Africa is the penannular pin, a kind of safety-pin often used to support heavy necklaces and other ornaments.

(4) Woman's headcover, Yemen, 20th cent.

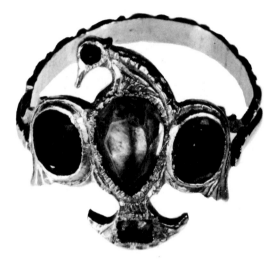

Above: (8) Woman's gold ring, Morocco, 19th cent.
Left: (6) Woman's dress, Morocco, 19th-20th cents.

Case (13) contains a reconstruction of the attire of a Jewish bride in San'a, Yemen. Though several different garments are worn during the two-week-long marriage celebration, this costume, worn for the final ceremony, is the most splendid, with its long, gold-brocade coat worn over two gowns and silver-embroidered leggings. The tall head-dress is embroidered with small pearls, coral, and glass beads, and rows of small filigree pendants, with other pendants at the sides. Strings of filigree beads hide the neck, and larger ones cover the front of the dress. Such magnificent costumes are occasionally still worn by Yemenite brides in Israel, though the celebrations themselves are considerably simpler than in the past.

Above: (14) Woman's breastpieces, East Europe, 19th cent.
Left: (5) Man's embroidered coat, Bokhara, 20th cent.

Passing cases (1-4) again, one leaves the main section of room 208 and comes to a triple case (14), containing various embroidered breast panels, pearl-work diadems, and bonnets in "spanier" work (a specific type of embroidery often seen on the edge of the *talit*, the man's prayer-shawl), worn by ashkenazi women in Eastern Europe in the 19th century.

45

Islamic Art

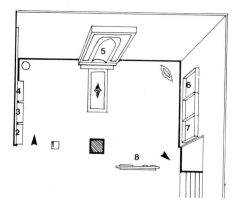

Stepping now into the Rabenou Gallery (room 209), one enters the realm of Islamic art. This department is currently being reorganized, and the display will eventually be concentrated in the archaeology section. Most of the display here is from the Persian artistic sphere.

Passing the freestanding case (1) with the fanciful 12th century incense burner in bronze from Iran — a fine example of early Islamic metalwork — we see three cases on the left containing various objects from Moghul India (16th-18th centuries) (2); from Safavid Iran (16th-18th centuries) (3); Mamluk Egypt or Syria (14th-15th centuries) (4); and a Timurid vase (No. 4, 15th century) from Iran.

On the adjacent wall (5), the large tiled *mihrab* (prayer niche) and the long inscription above it were made in Isfahan in the 17th century. Note that each piece of tile is shaped according to the design rather than the pattern being made up of square, painted tiles. The rug at the base of the niche is also from 17th century Isfahan.

(1) Incense burner, Iran, 12th cent.

46

Above: (6) Rayy painted cup, Iran, 12th-13th cents.
Right: (8) Safavid silver door, Iran, 17th cent.

In case (6), at the bottom right (Nos. 5 and 12) are a
Persian plate and pitcher of delicate beauty, painted in
the Minai style of the 12th-13th centuries, with minia-
tures of horsemen and other figures in full color.
In case (7), at the bottom we see the ornamental use of
decorative Arabic script painted on pottery of the 9th
century from Iran or Mesopotamia.
On the adjacent panel (8) is a pair of small doors made
of silver; their carpet pattern is typical of the Safavid
style of 17th century Iran.

Descending the stairs into room 210, one enters the
section of fine arts. Most of the museum's collection of
paintings, prints, drawings, and sculpture has been
acquired since the early 1930s through the generosity
of its benefactors in many countries. Not all these
works can be shown at one time, and changes are
occasionally made in the displays.

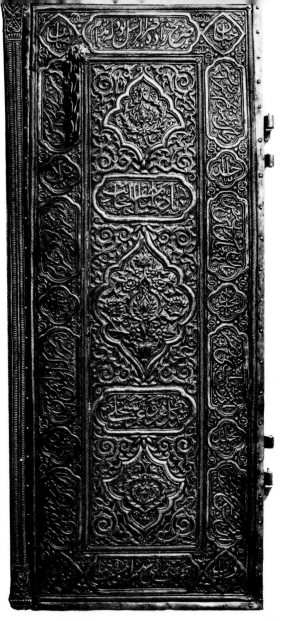

47

Prints and Drawings

Goya: "Capean Otro Encerrado" from Tauromaquia (1814).

Turn to the right into the I.M. Cohen Gallery for Prints and Drawings, to see the current exhibition. The department of prints and drawings organizes six to eight exhibitions annually, either from the museum's collections or from material received on loan. Major exhibitions have included the "Graphic Works of Pablo Picasso" (1972-73); "Herald of a New Age: Goya's Work" (1975); "Old Master Drawings from the Collec-tion of the Duke of Devonshire" (1977); and "Ingres: 53 Drawings from Life and Nature" (1981).

The museum's collection of prints and drawings contains some 50,000 items. The Old Masters collection, represented mainly by Italian, French and Netherland-ish artists, is highlighted by a drawing by Rembrandt and includes numerous prints by Albrecht Dürer

49

Above: Louis: Iota (1960-1).
Previous page: Mihrab (Islamic prayer niche), Isfahan, Persia, 17th cent.

Zaritsky: Painting, 1950-1

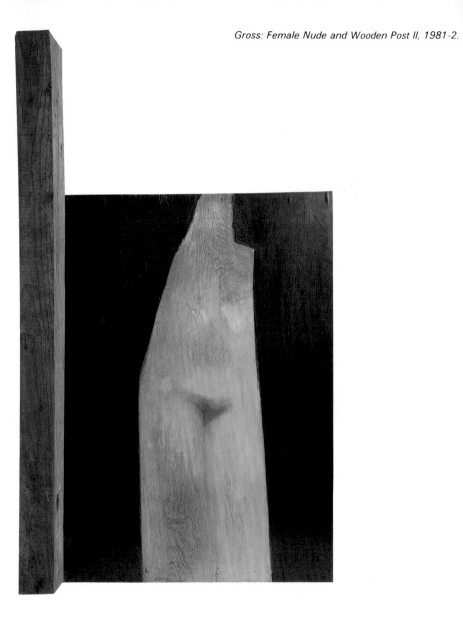

The large and representative collection of prints and drawings by Israeli artists includes works by Yosef Zaritsky, Anna Ticho (the museum has received her entire artistic legacy), Avigdor Arikha and many others. Specialized sections within the collection focus upon artists' book illustrations; Jewish subjects; and views of the Holy Land and Jerusalem.

Above: Anonymous: Portrait of Nobleman, Italy, 16th cent.
Right: Arikha: Portrait of Samuel Beckett (1970).

(woodcuts and engravings) and Francisco Goya (including the *Caprichos, Disasters of War* and *Tauromaquia*). Later artists represented include Auguste Rodin, Edgar Degas, Henri de Toulouse-Lautrec, Johan Barthold Jongkind, Fernand Léger, Marc Chagall, Jacques Lipchitz, Joan Miró, Paul Signac, Lyonel Feininger, Camille Pissarro and Vincent van Gogh; Paul Klee (eleven drawings, presented to the museum by Jan Mitchell of New York); and Jules Pascin (a unique group of about a hundred drawings, most of which were given by the artist's brother). Contemporary artists represented are Robert Rauschenberg, Jasper Johns, Jim Dine, Joe Tilson, Roy Lichtenstein, Andy Warhol and others.

Israeli Art

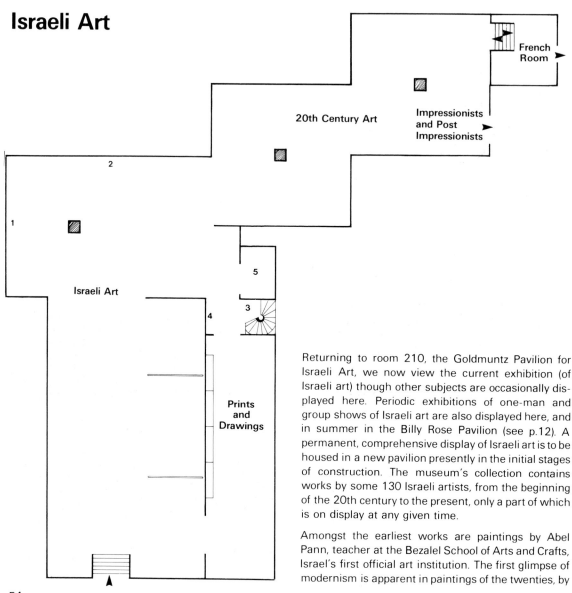

French Room

20th Century Art

Impressionists and Post Impressionists

2

1

5

Israeli Art

4

3

Prints and Drawings

Returning to room 210, the Goldmuntz Pavilion for Israeli Art, we now view the current exhibition (of Israeli art) though other subjects are occasionally displayed here. Periodic exhibitions of one-man and group shows of Israeli art are also displayed here, and in summer in the Billy Rose Pavilion (see p.12). A permanent, comprehensive display of Israeli art is to be housed in a new pavilion presently in the initial stages of construction. The museum's collection contains works by some 130 Israeli artists, from the beginning of the 20th century to the present, only a part of which is on display at any given time.

Amongst the earliest works are paintings by Abel Pann, teacher at the Bezalel School of Arts and Crafts, Israel's first official art institution. The first glimpse of modernism is apparent in paintings of the twenties, by

toward abstract art in the fifties and sixties is demonstrated in the works of numerous painters, including Yosef Zaritsky, Avigdor Stematsky, Yehezkel Streichman, Arie Aroch and Marcel Janco, as well as of the younger artists Lea Nikel and Ya'acov Agam; other trends are seen in the works of Yigael Tumarkin, Avraham Ofek, Raffi Lavie and Uri Lifshitz. The collection has been kept up-to-date by yearly purchases of works by avant-garde artists such as Joshua Neustein, Moshe Gershuni, Michael Gitlin, Pinhas Cohen Gan, Tamar Getter and Benni Efrat, and of works by the younger generation of new artists. Drawings by such fine Israeli draftsmen as Leopold Krakauer, Anna Ticho and Aviva Uri are often also shown.

Left: Gutman: Arab Boy Playing Flute (1928).
Below: Janco: Bal à Zurich (1917).

such artists as Haim Gliksberg, Arieh Lubin, Reuven Rubin, Nahum Gutman, Israel Paldi and Sionah Tagger. Works by Jacob Steinhardt and Mordechai Ardon are indicative of the importance of the German immigration of the thirties. In that same decade the integration of influences absorbed in Paris by many local artists is reflected in paintings by Pinhas Litvinovsky, Moshe Castel and others. The strong trend

Ticho: Judean Hills (1970s).

Above: Cohen-Gan: Landscape (1972).
Right: Danziger: Nimrod (1939).

Beyond, in room 212, on the left is (1) Mordechai Ardon's *At the Gates of Jerusalem* (1967), a kabbalistic triptych: (a) *Sign;* (b) *Ladders;* and (c) *Rock.* On the far wall (2) is Yosef Zaritsky's *Painting* (1967).

The *Graphics Study Room* is reached by descending the circular stairway (3). Opposite the stairway is the Kramer Corner for the graphic works of M.C. Escher (4).

The Memorial Room for Jewish Artists who Perished in the Holocaust (5) was installed through the generosity of the Gruss family of New York. Most of the works of the Jewish artists who perished during the Second World War have been lost, and the small part which survived is scattered throughout the world. This room displays a selection of such works, reflecting both European life between the two world wars and the Holocaust itself. Video programs in English and Hebrew provide 25 minutes of background material and insights into some of these artists and their work.

Above: (5) De Mesquita (1868-1944): Figures in a Row. Below: (4) Escher: Reptiles (1943).

20th Century Art

Dubuffet: Logologie (1974).

The next two rooms (213-214) contain contemporary art from the museum's collections with some loans and works by annual guest artists. The collection is constantly increasing in scope and with the limited space available it is difficult to show a comprehensive display. Various works of contemporary art are shown in other parts of the museum as well and the collection contains paintings of significance and quality, as well as many works showing unexpected or unfamiliar aspects of various schools and trends. Emphasis is on modern Western art, with examples from the Cubist, Surrealist, Expressionist and European and American Abstract movements as well as the more contemporary Op, Pop, Conceptual and Post-conceptual art.

There are important works by Georges Braque, Fernand Léger, Pablo Picasso, René Magritte, Paul Delvaux, Albert Gleizes and many others from the first half of the 20th century. Among works created after the Second World War, there are paintings by Francis Bacon, Karel Appel, Pierre Alechinsky, Jean Dubuffet, Willem de Kooning, Adolph Gottlieb, Helen Frankenthaler, Morris Louis, Philip Guston, Sam Francis, Andy Warhol, Jim Dine, Tom Wesselman, Bridget Riley, Agnes Martin and several other important artists. Temporary exhibitions are a central aspect of the

Above: Léger: Figure Composition (1924).
Opp: Bacon: Study for Portrait of Lucien Freud (1964).

department's activities. One-man shows of artists of international stature, such as Morris Louis and Sam Francis, are annual events. In addition, the museum invites one artist a year from abroad to exhibit and this is usually shown in the Billy Rose Pavilion. Dennis Oppenheim, Joel Shapiro and Deborah Butterfield are among the artists who have participated within this framework. The department also mounts thematic exhibitions from its collections.

Impressionists and Post- Impressionists

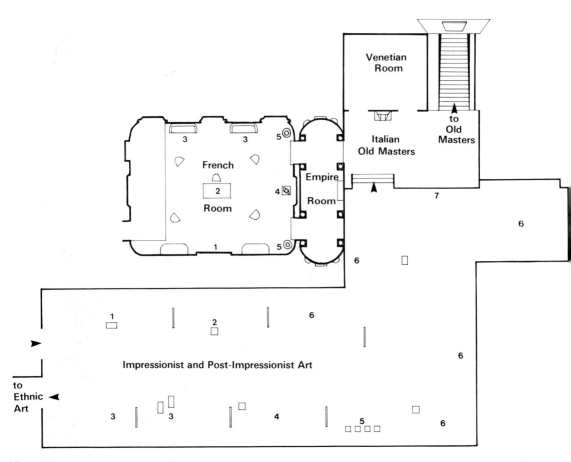

Venetian
Room

to
Old
Masters

Italian
Old Masters

French

Empire

Room

Room

Impressionist and Post-Impressionist Art

to
Ethnic
Art

Entering the Floersheimer Pavilion for Impressionist and Post-Impressionist Art (room 105), one finds oneself in a large, naturally-lit space. The specially-designed ceiling provides the feeling of being in the open air, so vital to the Impressionist paintings on view here.

On the left-hand wall are several paintings by precursors of Impressionism (1): Jean Baptiste Camille Corot, Gustave Courbet and several works by Eugène Boudin (notably *The Sea at St. Vaast-la-Hougue*). In the adjacent freestanding case is a terracotta by Jules Dalou, *Woman Reading*, sculpted in 1871. On the adjacent panel is Edouard Vuillard's *The Chaise Longue*, a fine Post-Impressionist painting.

The next group of paintings (2) represents artists from various countries who brought the impact of French Impressionism to their native lands: the Russian-Jewish landscape painter Isaak Ilyich Levitan, whose life was cut short at the age of forty; the German-Jewish artists Max Liebermann and Lesser Ury; and the American Childe Hassam. Edgar Degas' small bronze *Dancer* is displayed in the adjacent freestanding case.

Turning back now to the right-hand wall, one sees Impressionist paintings including works by Camille Pissarro and Alfred Sisley, Claude Monet's *Haystacks,* and Paul Cézanne's *Country House by a River*. Auguste Renoir's bronze sculptures *Fire* and *Water* stand nearby.

The Post-Impressionist works on view (4) include several paintings and a small bronze by Paul Gauguin, paintings by his disciples Paul Sérusier and Emile Bernard *(Portrait of Marie Lemasson)* and two landscapes by Vincent van Gogh. Auguste Rodin's four bronzes, *the Titans,* are displayed just beyond (5).

(1) Dalou: Woman Reading (1871).

Toward the farther end of the room are works by 20th century artists (6). Artists who worked in Paris early in the century are shown here, including Maurice de Vlaminck, Maurice Utrillo, Henri Matisse, Marc Chagall *(The Rabbi),* Georges Rouault, Jules Pascin and Chaim Soutine *(The Hill at Céret).* Sculpture by Matisse is also on view. The German and Austrian Expressionist works on display (7) include paintings by Max Pechstein, Egon Schiele (*City,* 1915), and Oskar Kokoschka *(Portrait of Professor Leo Kestenberg).*

Schiele: City (1915)

Victors: Dismissal of Hagar (1650).

(3) Renoir: Faubourg de Maintenon (1888).

Empire-Style Room

18th Cent. French Room

Descending several steps into room 217, one turns to the left and enters the Empire-style room (215) containing the John Simons Collection of early 19th century porcelain. The Empire style, which developed out of Neo-Classicism, flourished under Napoleon I and during the Bourbon restoration (1804-1830). Most of the pieces on display here were made at Sèvres or at other French factories. The painting on display in this room, *Three Ladies Decorating a Statue of Cupid with Garlands of Flowers*, is by Marguerite Gérard. The room was designed and donated by Henri Samuel, who was responsible for the installation of the 18th century French period room which can be seen through the doorway.

This interior, the gift of the Baron and Baroness Edmond de Rothschild, was originally the grand salon of an aristocrat's house in the Faubourg Saint-Germain in Paris, built in 1740-45 for Samuel Bernard, Comte de Coubert. He inherited a vast fortune which he squandered within a few years, and had to sell his beautiful house. This room was dismantled in the 1880s, when the house was demolished; it was then installed in the Rothschild home in Paris, where it is said to have been the study of the first Baron Edmond. It was again dismantled after the Second World War, and installed in the museum in 1968-69. The original house, including this room, was designed in the Rococo style. The magnificent white and gilt carved panels are reminiscent of similar panelling at Versailles. Over the doors are painted depictions of the four continents (Asia, Africa, Europe and America) by Jean Restout, Jean Dumont and Charles Vanloo.

The room contains 18th century works of art and furnishings, also presented by Baron and Baroness de Rothschild. The fine mantlepiece on the left is flanked by two tapestries made by Cozette at the Royal Gobelin Manufactory in Paris, after paintings by Hallé *(Silenus and Aegle)* and Vien *(The Rape of Proserpine)*. At the center of the room is a Louis XV desk, with a fine pair of Sèvres vases and around the desk are five Louis XV armchairs, upholstered with Gobelin tapestries. On the right-hand wall, between the windows, are two portraits : *Marguerite-Françoise Dupleix de Bacquencourt* by Jacques Aved; and *Portrait of Madame de Laporte as Diana* by Jean-Marc Nattier. Both ladies are portrayed in the year of their marriage — the former aged 20 and the latter, 17. Against the near wall is a marble statue, *Diana with a Hunting Horn*, by Guillaume Coustou I. In the near corners are two Chinese Ch'ien Lung porcelain vases .

Italian Pavilion

Leaving the Empire-style room, one re-enters the Schapira Italian Art Pavilion (room 217). Between the two doorways on the left is a carved and inlaid walnut secrétaire of the 18th century from Venice. From the flanking doorways we can see into an 18th century room, probably from a Venetian palace, donated by Mr. and Mrs. Renato Bacchi of Milan, and installed in 1975. The *chinoiserie* ornamentation is in a fashion which swept Europe in the 18th century. In the niches on the far wall are two *papier mâché* figures of a

Chinoiserie room, Venice, 18th cent.

Chinese man and woman with nodding heads, also from Venice. The design of the carved and painted wood candelabrum, which also contains a two-faced clock, has been attributed to Tiepolo. The carpet is Chinese.

On view in the main pavilion are paintings by such 17th and 18th century Italian painters as Alessandro Magnasco, Giovanni Antonio Pellegrini (*Danaë*, over the doorway to the Empire room), Nicola Grassi *(The Finding of Moses)*, Paolo de Matteis (after Luca Giordano, *The Song of Miriam*) and, over the descending staircase, Bernardo Strozzi *(St. Peter Performing a Miracle)*.

Opp. Right: Strozzi, St. Peter Performing Miracle, 17th cent.
Above: Giordano: The Song of Miriam, 17th cent.

Old Masters

Down the long stairway, one reaches the Nash Old Masters Gallery. The museum's collection of Old Master paintings, a small part of which has just been seen in the Italian art pavilion, includes a number of fine works by well-known artists from various schools.

At the bottom of the stairs are two paintings (1) which demonstrate the skill of the Dutch in the 17th century in still-life and genre paintings (Cornelis de Heem, *A Vase of Flowers*, and Pieter Cornilis van Slingelandt, *The Tailor's Workshop*). On the wall to the left are paintings (2) by Anthony van Dyck *(Portrait of the Engraver Paulus Pontius)*, Gabriel Metsu *(The Sacrifice of Isaac)*, Rembrandt van Rijn *(The Apostle James, 1661* — on extended loan to the museum), and Govaert Flinck, Rembrandt's pupil *(Venus and Cupid)*.

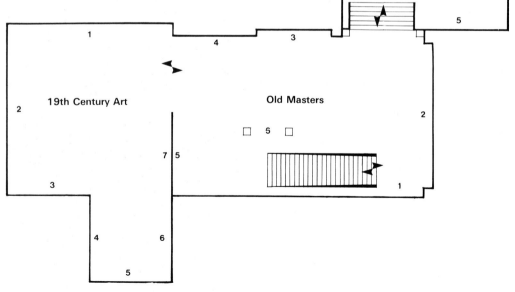

English Dining Room

Descending the adjacent steps into room 220, and crossing over to the right-hand doorway (1) on the opposite wall, one reaches the Ida Berg 18th Century English Dining Room donated by her son, David Berg of New York. This pine-paneled room contains period furniture, silver, porcelain and other furnishings. The majestic gilt-wood chandelier (a) is of the George I period. The Adam side-table (b) on the far wall is from about 1775, and on it, amongst many other articles, is a pair of urn-shaped wooden Sheraton knife-boxes made around 1795. Above the side-table is a portrait by George Romney, painted in 1784. Against the right-hand wall is a pair of George I gilt-gesso side-tables (c). The pair of mirrors with candlesticks, above, are Irish. The porcelain on the shelves (d) flanking the mantle-piece, on the left-hand wall, is English Chelsea ware. Between the two doorways on the near wall is a fine carved and gilt Chippendale mirror (e).

The outstanding feature of this room is the splendid array of 18th century English silver, much of it made by the best London silversmiths, including such well-known artisans as Paul de Lamerie, the Bateman family, Francis Garthorne, William Pitt, William Cafe and, especially, Paul Storr.

Again in room 220, the central case (2) contains several examples of English silver which can be examined from close up, including a large monteith (a sort of punch-bowl) in Queen Anne style, made in London in 1705 (note the grotesque lion's mask forming the back-plate of each handle.

Turning back to the far corner (3), one re-enters the realm of the Old Masters: the still-life *Vanitas* was painted by the Flemish artist Cornelis Norbertus Gysbrechts in 1667. On the adjacent wall (4) are two Dutch landscapes: *River Landscape with a City Gate* (1644) by Jan van Goyen, and *Landscape by Moonlight* (1646)

(3) J.G. and A. Cuyp: Portrait of a Family (1641).

by Aert van der Neer. On the wall to the right (5) is *David with the Head of Goliath*, by an unknown painter of the school of Utrecht, and a detail-laden *Tavern Scene* by Jacob Duck.

Crossing over to (6) one sees a *Landscape with a View of Het Steen* by Lucan van Uden, a 17th century Flemish artist of the circle of Rubens. On the adjacent wall (7) is the meticulous *Interior of Antwerp Cathedral* by Pieter Neefs the Elder, another 17th century Flemish

artist. Next to this is *The Conjurer*, a moralizing fantasy based on a painting by Hieronymus Bosch; note the pickpocket on the left.

Re-entering the Nash Old Masters Gallery, on the right is (3) *Portrait of a Family in a Landscape*, painted by the portraitist Jacob Gerritsz Cuyp and his famous landscape-painter son Aelbert in 1641. The age of each member of the family is recorded beneath the

(6) Enamelled casket (detail), Limoges, 16th cent. France.

figures (except for the servants, at either side). Beyond this work is a pair of biblical paintings by the Italian Giacinto Gimignani (4): *The Triumph of David* and *The Death of Absalom*, with many features harking back to Classical art. Crossing the room to (5), one sees the *Martyrdom of a Saint* by Monsu Desiderio (Francois Nomé) and, next to it, the Dutchman Jan Victors' *Dismissal of Hagar*, dated 1650.

Other Old Masters represented in the museum collection include the Dutch painters Allaert van Everdingen, Paulus Potter, Cornelis Janssens and Johannes Cor-nelisz. Verspronck, and the Flemish artist Jan Miel *(The Crossing of the Red Sea)*.

In the two freestanding cases (6) are an enameled casket from 16th century Limoges, depicting scenes from the story of Joseph; a round, gilt plaque from 17th century Germany, depicting Abraham and the Three Angels; and a splendid pair of silver-gilt goblets from 17th century Nuremberg, depicting scenes from Genesis. There were at least two more cups in the set, for the scenes are numbered: 4-6, *Cain and Abel*, *Noah's Ark*, and *The Flood*; and 10-12, *Lot's Daughters*, *Sarah and the Angel*, and *The Sacrifice of Isaac*.

75

19th Century Art

(1) Lear: Jerusalem from Mount of Olives (1858).

Beyond, we enter the gallery of 19th Century Art, opened in 1981, with works reflecting various trends, such as Biedermeier, the Pre-Raphaelites, Academicism and Realism. Several of these artists were Jewish, and some were subsequently influenced by the Impressionists and are thus also represented in the Impressionist pavilion upstairs.

Edward Lear, the British artist and nonsense poet, and

the Frenchman Jean-Léon Gérôme both visited the Holy Land in the mid 19th century, and their paintings shown here (1) — Lear's two landscapes and Gérôme's *The Wailing Wall* (based on sketches made on the spot) give faithful renderings of the country as they saw it. Several paintings by the Dutch-Jewish artist Jozef Israels are shown on the adjacent wall (2), including a fine self-portrait and a larger work entitled *Saying Grace* which may have influenced Van Gogh's

two highly divergent paintings by Moritz Oppenheim (6), whose series on Jewish themes is a most important documentation of ashkenazi life; his *Kindling the Hanukkah Lights* (1880) gives many details of a Jewish home; his *Portrait of a Young Lady* (1825) is the earliest painting shown in this gallery. Beyond are (7) *Two Views of a Farm* by Isidor Kaufmann, framed together; two paintings by the German artist Karl Spitzweg; and another well-known Daumier bronze, *Le Ratapoil*.

From here one returns to the upper level, crosses the Impressionist pavilion and enters the Maremont Pavilion of Ethnic Art (through the left-hand doorway).

Above: (4) Daumier: Caricatures in bronze (1830-32).
Right: (5) Gottlieb (1856-79): Jewish Wedding.

Potato Eaters. Nearby are works by several artists also represented upstairs: Max Liebermann, Lesser Ury and Isaak Levitan; Levitan's *Zvenigrod Monastery* (3) is an outstanding, powerfully beautiful landscape.

The series of caricature heads in bronze (4) are by Honoré Daumier. Beyond are two paintings by Eugène Carrière, in his typically veiled style. Maurycy Gottlieb's *Portrait of a Young Woman* and *Jewish Wedding* (5) reveal the talent of this Polish-Jewish artist, who died in 1879 at the age of twenty-three. Adjacent are

Pavilion of Ethnic Art

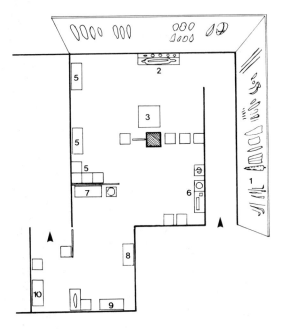

Opp. Left: (9) Grave-post, Dyak people, Borneo.
Opp. Right: (3) Female figure, Lower Sepik Papua-New Guinea.

podium (3) are several wooden figures, one of which has a most interestingly styled head. There are ancestor boards on the wall to the left and above the drums (4), from the Sepik river region; they are a sort of heraldic device, much like the coats-of-arms of medieval Europe, whose patterns reveal familial relationships. The subsequent cases (5) show additional everyday and ceremonial objects from Papua-New Guinea.

Section (6) displays Melanesian objects from New Britain, east of New Guinea; from New Caledonia and from the New Hebrides Islands, some 2,000 kilometers to the southeast. On the left-hand podium is a friction-drum of interesting form, while in the cases to the right are two large masks, one made of bark cloth.

Crossing over to case (7), one sees various objects from Polynesia, many of them finely carved. Note the Maori cloak and canoe-bailer from New Zealand on the right. At (8), opposite, there is a small group of boomerangs and other objects of Australian aboriginal art. In adjacent case (9) are objects from other eastern Pacific islands. Note the carved wooden hat from Taiwan, at the top left; the musket-ball holders from Sumatra, on the upper right; and the finely carved weaving shuttle from Borneo, at the bottom.

Case (10) contains a small number of objects from North America, from the Pacific Northwest coast (Eskimo), the Plains (Cheyenne and Nez Percé) and the Southwest (a kachina doll of the Pueblo Indians).

The next gallery, intended for African art, is currently used for temporary exhibitions from the ethnic art collections.

The Maremont ethnic art pavilion, opened in 1979, encompasses the art of Oceania, Africa and the Americas — material seldom seen on display in Israel. A section on African art is still in the planning stage.

The Wright Gallery of Oceanic and American Indian Art was inaugurated late in 1980. On the right-hand wall as you enter (1) are weapons and shields from various areas of the Pacific.

The next section of the display is devoted to Papua-New Guinea. The carved slit-drum (2) measures two and a half meters and was used for sending messages or summoning meetings, while the adjacent hand-drums were used as musical instruments. On the

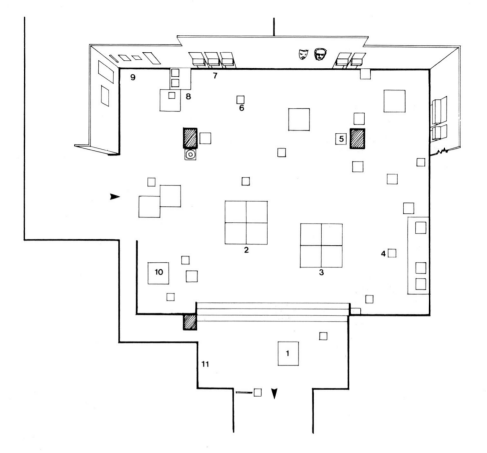

Entering room 103 from the side, we enter an exhibition on "The Human Image in Pre-Columbian Art" from Central and South America. The display seeks to emphasize the artistic stability and continuity found in the vast area and extended time-span encompassed by the term "pre-Columbian" — despite its diversity of styles, meanings and functions. Crossing over to the starting-point of the exhibition, and up several steps to (1), the display is dominated by the splendid figure of a seated man with a jaguar head emerging from his torso, from Veracruz, Mexico, around 600-900 CE.

On the central podium (2) are several outstanding figures, including a seated woman holding a rattle and a bowl (No. 63, on the right, behind), from Jalisco in western Mexico, around 100 CE; and a seated woman with her head resting on her knee (No. 65, on the right, in front), also from Jalisco, around 100 BCE — 100 CE. To the right, on podium (3), amongst various figures is

(2) Figure with jaguar head, Veracruz, Mexico, 600-900 CE.

Just beyond is a group of Peruvian pottery (8), mostly from tombs and especially made for funerary use. Indeed, in most of the art represented by the objects on display, death appears as a recurrent theme. Outstanding in this group of pottery is a vase in the form of a head (No. 117, near the wall), from the 3rd-6th centuries CE. In the corner beyond is a selection of Peruvian textiles (9), remarkable products of the weaver's art from 300 BCE on.

Turning back to podium (10), one finds among other figures from Central America, a standing figure in curious, barbed dress (No. 101), from Ecuador, 500 BCE — 500 CE.

Above the steps, on the right, is a large gold burial mask (11) from Peru (1300-1476 CE), a stylization of man and wealth in death.

Smiling face, Veracruz, Mexico, 600-900 CE.

No. 13 (in the center), a cylindrical incense burner depicting Tlaloc, the rain god of the Toltecs of western Mexico, from around 100 CE.

The smiling face in case (4) — possibly that of Xochipilli, god of dance — is from Veracruz, Mexico, from around 600-900 CE. In case (5) is a very impressive standing figure (No. 85, on the right), from Guerro, Mexico, from around 1200-100 BCE. In case (6), a standing figure (No. 28, from the Valley of Mexico) is holding a mask to its face (450-100 BCE), and on the far wall is a group of small masks (7) from Mexico, including an especially delightful one (No. 33) made of mottled green stone, from 300-100 BCE.

Far Eastern Art

The department of Far Eastern art is currently building up its collections, the core of which was formed by the Wolf Ladejinsky Bequest. The collection includes material dating from 1300 BCE to the 20th century: Chinese, Korean, Thai and Vietnamese ceramics, Indian and other southeast Asian bronzes and stone sculpture, and Indian and Tibetan paintings. The Chinese pottery consists mainly of early pieces of the Han to Sung dynasties (early 3rd century BCE to 13th century CE), and there are several notable early Chinese bronzes of the Shang period (15th-11th centuries BCE). The Thai pottery represents a comprehensive group from the 14th-15th centuries, including several unique pieces.

Recent exhibitions have included "The Pins Collection: Chinese and Japanese Paintings and Prints"; "Studies in Connoisseurship; Chinese Paintings from the Arthur M. Sackler Collection"; and "Asian Art from the Wolf Ladejinsky Collection".

Tang Mirror, China, 618-906 CE.

Photography

The Israel Museum has exhibited photographs ever since its opening, but the department of photography was established only in 1977 and as yet has no permanent exhibition area of its own. Its growing collection includes over 4,000 photographs and is the largest in Israel; it covers almost the entire history of photography, from early daguerreotypes through the major 19th century photographers (Talbot, Nadar, Cameron) to modern artists such as Man Ray, Arnold Newman, André Kertész and Ansel Adams. A strong feature is the collection of early photographs of the Holy Land, taken from 1839 on, representing the major photographers who worked in Israel. The department also possesses most of the oeuvre of the pioneer Israeli photographer Yaacov Ben-Dov (1,400 glass negatives and a similar number of prints). An important realm of interest for the department is contemporary Israeli photography. This is complemented by a small collection of antique cameras and equipment.

Major exhibitions have included "Arnold Newman — Portrait Photographs" (1978); "Photographs from the Dan Berley Collection, New York" (1980); "André Kertész: Photographs of a Lifetime" (1980); and "The Third Dimension — Laser Photography" (1981).

The collection is available to the public by special arrangement for purposes of research and study.

Numismatic Gallery

Flanking the entrance are two cases containing Jewish commemorative medallions (1). In the case to the right, the following subjects are illustrated:

Jewish emancipation: No. 3 was issued by Napoleon Bonaparte in commemoration of the "Sanhedrin" of Jews which he established in 1806.

Zionism: No. 2, designed by Samuel Friedrich Beer (Paris, 1898), was issued in commemoration of the second Zionist congress in Basel.

Miscellaneous: No. 1 was issued in commemoration of the 250th anniversary of the first settlement of Jews in North America; No. 2 was issued by French Jewry to honor Napoleon III in 1870; and No. 3 bears a fine portrait of Rachel (Elisa-Rachel Felix, 1821-1858), the famous Jewish actress of the Comédie Francaise.

Marriage: Nos. 1-2 are late 19th century German medals commemorating specific Jewish weddings.

Burial Societies: Such hand-engraved tokens would be bought from the benevolent societies and given to the poor, who would then submit them back to the societies in order to receive material support.

Circumcision: This early Dutch medal was cast in gold in 1665, on the occasion of the birth of a boy named David.

Anti-Semitism: Many medals were issued from the early 16th century onward — almost all in Germany. No. 1, in the form of a small box, portrays Joseph Süsskind Oppenheimer (*Jew Süss* — finance minister in Württemberg) and the scaffold on which he was hanged in 1738. Within is a series of 19 depictions of his life, from birth to tragic death. No. 2 depicts the *Korn Jude*, the "grain Jew" — seeking to show the Jews as profiteers during hard times (issued from the late 17th century till the 1770s). No. 5, issued after the extensive fires of 1721 in Frankfurt, Germany, accuses the Jews of being responsible for them. No. 7 concerns

(1) "Jud Süss" medal, Germany, mid-18th cent.

the Dreyfus affair, in which a Jewish captain in the French army was unjustly convicted of treason in 1894; he was later pardoned and the charges proven false. No. 8 commemorates Menachem Mendel Beilis, charged with the ritual murder of a Christian boy in Kiev, Ukraine, in 1913; this was the last major blood-libel trial against a Jew. Beilis was acquitted.

In the left-hand case, Jewish communities and personalities are commemorated.

Synagogues: In Germany (Nos. 1-7), Italy (No. 8), Holland (Nos. 9-11), Hungary (No. 12) and Rumania (No. 13).

Jewish personalities: No. 2, Gracia Nasi (cast, Italy, 1558 — the earliest clearly Jewish medal with a Hebrew inscription); No. 4, the 17th century philosopher Baruch Spinoza (Holland); No. 5, the philosopher Moses Mendelssohn (by the German-Jewish medallist Jacob Abraham, 1722-1800); No. 8, coat-of-arms of the house of Rothschild (Germany, 1844); Nos. 9-12, Sir Moses Montefiore, 19th century British philanthropist; No. 16, Dr. Isaac Mannheimer (Austria, 1863 — the die for this medallion is also in the museum collection).

Ancient Coins

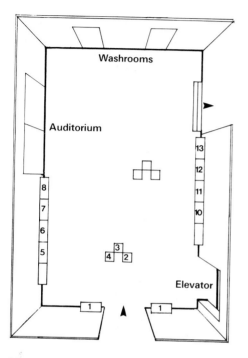

From above left, clockwise: (5) "Yehud", 4th cent. BCE; (10) Hasmonean 37 BCE; (11) Temple coin, Bar Kokhba, 135 CE (11) "Judea Capta", 1st cent. CE.

Money means different things to different people: for the historian, coins are a record of nations and an insight into economic history; for the archaeologist, they provide a means of accurately dating discoveries; and for the connoisseur, they are gems of art, a delight to the eye. The display gives an outline of the coins used in Israel from the dawn of coinage to the present. A scene from the Bible — Noah's ark — uniquely appears on a Roman coin of the 3rd century CE (2), and a hoard of Tyrian and Jewish shekels (3), of the sort used in Herod's temple in Jerusalem, was found hidden within a fine bronze container. A pleasing portrait of king Agrippa I (4), Herod's grandson, is one of the few ancient depictions of a Jewish king.

The history of Jerusalem is reviewed in a series of coins (5) used there, from the Persian period (6th-4th centuries BCE) down through to Crusader times (12th-13th centuries CE). Note No. 1, which bears the legend "Yehud", the name of Judea under Persian rule, and No. 17, which has a Crusader depiction of the Holy Sepulcher.

The coins of the Near East in the Persian period (6) show influence of Greek art and represent a zenith in local coinage, approaching the level of beauty of the Greek masterpieces of minting in gold and silver (7).

The principles of minting coins (8) have changed little over the ages, though techniques have been mechanized and refined. Note the Early Arab (10th century CE) die (No. 1) alongside a modern Israeli die (No. 2).

In Old Testament times, before the introduction of coinage, wealth was often concentrated and hoarded in the form of jewelry (9).

Independent Jewish coinage, from the mid 2nd century BCE to the mid 2nd century CE, began with the Maccabean (10) and Herodian dynasties. Their coins were inscribed in Hebrew, Aramaic or Greek, and bore symbols which avoided offending Jewish religious sensitivities concerning graven images. Only in non-Jewish areas under Herodian control were coins issued with portraits (4).

With the outbreak of the great Jewish revolt against Rome, in 66 CE, the Jews asserted their autonomy by issuing large silver coins or "shekels" (11), bearing nationalistic motifs and such legends as: "Jerusalem the holy", "for the redemption of Zion" and "shekel of Israel". The Romans brutally suppressed this revolt (see p. 142) though one of their legions was decimated in the process. To mark their victory over the Jews the Romans issued *Judaea capta* (Judea vanquished) coins (11), showing Judea personified, lamenting her loss of freedom.

Sixty years later, during the reign of Hadrian, the Jews again tried to shake off the yoke of Rome. Then, too, they defiantly issued silver coins (12), also with nationalistic symbols and slogans. These were overstruck on Roman coins, and occasionally the emperor's portrait and part of his titles can be seen beneath the Jewish patterns. Some of these coins bear the name of the leader of the revolt: "Shimon (bar Kokhba)" (No. 3); others show the Jerusalem temple, which had been destroyed some sixty years earlier, (No. 11/2). The suppression of this revolt, in 135 CE, signalled the end of autonomous Jewish minting until the establishment of the state of Israel in 1948. The patterns on Israel's modern coins are mostly derived from ancient Jewish coins (13), as are the names of the denominations.

(3) Tyrian and Jewish shekel hoard, 68 CE.

Archaeology
The Samuel Bronfman Biblical Archaeological Museum

Entering the Goldman-Schwarz Hall once again, and crossing over to the left, to the stairs leading down into room 301 (Prehistory), we enter the archaeology section.

In Israel, the land of the Bible, archaeology has always been an emotionally charged field of interest, having special significance to the Jews as well as to Christians and Muslims. The galleries of the Samuel Bronfman Biblical and Archaeological Museum enable one to follow the course of Israel's history from prehistory through to the middle ages. Most of the objects on display are from archaeological excavations in Israel. They reflect the cultural history of the surrounding regions as well, as can be seen in the display on neighboring cultures in room 314, which assists in placing the archaeology of Israel in perspective.

The archaeological galleries are labelled according to periods and dates. The terminology adopted at the Israel Museum refers to the Bronze Age in Israel as the Canaanite Age, in deference to the dominant local culture of that period, just as the term Israelite Age is applied to the local Iron Age. The archaeological periods are summarized as follows, in accord with the displays in the galleries. Some of the exhibits in the archaeology section are in the process of change, and this guide may not always reflect the current display.

Chronological Chart

Prehistory

Paleolithic (Old Stone Age)	**1,000,000 — 18,000 BCE**
Lower Paleolithic	1,000,000 — 80,000 BCE
Middle Paleolithic	80,000 — 43,000 BCE
Upper Paleolithic	43,000 — 18,000 BCE
Epipaleolithic (Late Old Stone Age)	**18,000 — 8,300 BCE**
Kabaran culture	18,000 — 10,500 BCE
Natufian culture	10,500 — 8,300 BCE
Harifian culture	8,500 — 8,000 BCE
Neolithic (New Stone Age)	**8,300 — 4,000 BCE**
Pre-Pottery A	8,300 — 7,500 BCE
Pre-Pottery B	7,500 — 6.000 BCE
Early Pottery	6,000 — 5.000 BCE
Late Pottery	5,000 — 4,000 BCE

Historic Periods

Chalcolithic Age	**4,000 — 3,150 BCE**
Canaanite (Bronze) Age	**3,150 — 1,200 BCE**
Early Canaanite	3,150 — 2,200 BCE
Middle Canaanite I	2,200 — 2,000 BCE
Middle Canaanite II	2,000 — 1,500 BCE
Late Canaanite	1,500 — 1,200 BCE
Israelite (Iron) Age	**1,200 — 586 BCE**
Early Israelite	1,200 — 1,000 BCE
Late Israelite	1,000 — 586 BCE
Persian Period	**late 6th cent. BCE — late 4th cent. BCE**
Hellenistic Period	**late 4th cent. BCE — late 1st cent. BCE**
Roman Period	**late 1st cent. BCE — early 4th cent. CE**
Byzantine Period	**early 4th cent. CE — 638 CE**
Early Arab Period	**638 CE — 11th cent. CE**
Crusader Period	**12th cent. CE — 13th cent. CE**

Prehistory

(ca. 1,000,000 — 4,000 BCE)

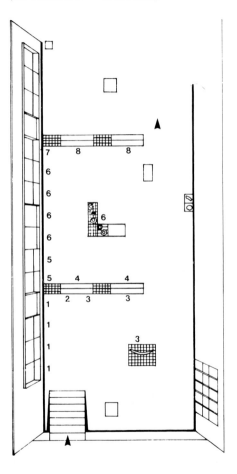

The earliest evidence of human activity in Israel goes back some one million years, though in East Africa human remains three or four million years old have been found — the earliest known appearance of man on earth. The geographical location of Israel made it a land-bridge between major continents, and thus it played a significant role in both natural and human history.

The Paleolithic period

(ca. 1,000,000 — ca. 18,000 BCE)

In *Lower Paleolithic* times major changes in the landscape were still taking place throughout Israel, and a moderate, somewhat humid climate prevailed. There were sweetwater lakes, swamps and springs; African-type fauna such as elephants, hippopotami, giraffes, large wild cattle and monkeys still roamed the land. Animals of northern origin were also to be seen, such as the roe-deer and bears. Man already possessed fire and the ability to form tools, probably of wood and certainly of stone, especially flint — as seen in the heavy handaxes in case. Toward the end of this period, man began dwelling in caves and new, flaked types of tools began to appear. The skull in case (2), found in the Zuttiye cave, represents the oldest human remains found in Israel.

The onset of the relatively short *Middle Paleolithic* period (3) is marked by a renewed cold climate, and the entire Jordan valley was a single, large salt lake. The mountains were forested and larger fauna of the African type had vanished. Man was able to settle even in today's arid desert regions — in the south (Negev) and in the east (Judean desert). He was further perfecting his tools, which he now often made of flakes of flint — scrapers, knives, burins and spearheads. Burials (3, Nos. 3-5 and lower right) now reveal specific attitudes

(2) Handaxes, Holon ca.300,000 BCE.

toward death — reflecting some form of spiritual belief in an afterlife. The skeletal remains indicate two types of man here: *homo sapiens* with Neanderthaloid affinities, and modern *homo sapiens*.

Upper Paleolithic times (4) began with a rainy period followed by a cold, dry climate, Mediterranean-type forests still covered large tracts of the land, and fallow deer were commonly hunted. Dwelling-sites are found from northern Israel down to Sinai — in caves, in rock shelters and in the open. Further technical developments were made in flint tool manufacture, and bone tools and some limestone and basalt grinding implements appear toward the end of the period. Modern *homo sapiens* had prevailed.

Epipaleolithic period
(18,000 — 8,300 BCE)

The period of the *Kabaran culture* (5) — first found in the Kabara Cave on Mount Carmel, hence its name, was cold and damp, with lakes and swamps scattered throughout the northern part of the country; the Negev had sparse, open forests where gazelles, ostriches and ibex were still being hunted. Many of the flint blades of this period are tiny (microliths), and must have been set into handles or shafts, forming harpoons and other developed weapons and tools. Cereals were gathered from the wild, and grinding, baking and cooking are shown to have existed by the presence of stone mortars and pestles as well as other finds. Fishing and fowling probably supplemented the bland daily fare.

The *Natufian culture* (6) — first found in Wadi Natuf in the western Judean hills — also flourished in a damp climate, and even the Negev was inhabited. A broad scope of human activities is indicated by villages with circular dwellings and various household installations, as well as by the variety of tools. The latter include hunting, fishing and harvesting implements, mortars and pestles, and flint and bone tools. Now we begin finding bone and stone carvings representing animals (7), and even schematic human representations (7, upper center). Bone, stone and shell jewelry is occasionally discovered in graves which are often located within the settlements themselves — some of the materials used pointing to primitive trade with distant regions. The dominant human type now was Mediterranean in build and features.

The *Harifian culture* (9) — first discovered at Mount Harif in the Negev highlands — continued the Natufian tradition but was limited to the arid zones of the country, typified by microlithic tools and round dwellings with various household installations.

Above right: (11) Stone figurines, left: Nahal Oren ca. 8000
BCE, right: Salabia ca. 8300 BCE.
Above right: (11) Stone figurines, Salatiah ca. 8300 BCE.
Right: (14) Plastered skull Beisamun ca. 6500 BCE.
Opp: Bone sickle handle in animal shape, Natufian Period.

The Neolithic period
(8,300 — 4,000 BCE)

In early Neolithic times, too, the climate was more humid than it is today. Early in this period we see man's first steps in agriculture (10). And towards the end of the period he learned to make vessels of clay. The latter invention has led prehistorians to divide this period into "pre-pottery" and "pottery" phases.

In the *Pre-Pottery A* phase, dwellings were still round (11), and late in the phase, for the first time, we see settlements surrounded by walls such as at Jericho. Some of the axes were polished, sickle-blades took on new forms and arrowheads first appear in large quanti-ties. Querns (grinding stones) and small mortars were new features. Trade with the Anatolia region is now seen, with the appearance locally of obsidian (volcanic glass), used for making tools and weapons.

In the *Pre-Pottery B* phase, which we find represented on numerous sites, rectangular structures now appeared, though in the Negev round houses continued to be built. The flint tools were of high quality, especially the arrowheads. Of special note are human and animal figurines moulded of clay or carved in stone (13), and at several sites, from late in the phase, skulls have been found beneath the floors of the houses, plastered over and modelled with the features of the

Opp: Copper objects from Cave of the Treasure, Judean Desert, second half, 4th. Mill.
Below: (16) Painted and incised pottery, Sha'ar Hagolan and H. Minha, 6th mill.

deceased (14). Now, too, there was clear evidence throughout the ancient Near East of the domestication of sheep and goats, as well as the cultivation of indigenous cereals and pulses.

In the earlier part of the *Pottery Neolithic*, most dwellings were in the form of huts or pits. Earlier use of clay now led to the discovery that pottery could be baked, creating durable, strong vessels. Such pottery (17) allowed for the storage of surplus foodstuffs, and made cooking much easier. Larger cattle and pigs were now also domesticated. The pottery vessels of the Yarmukian culture, in the northern valley, were globular or straight-sided, and often were decorated with incised lines or herringbone patterns, with the flat areas between them painted red (12). The associated figurines (15) are quite remarkable, and some unknown cult urge undoubtedly underlies their creation. Here, too, toothed sickle-blades provide evidence of agricultural activity.

In the *Late Pottery Neolithic* period, as earlier, the settled area was mostly confined to the zone of Mediterranean climate but toward the end of the period settlement expanded into the arid regions. Generally, buildings were now rectangular in plan and set on stone foundations. Agriculture became more intensive, and a variety of pottery shapes appears, with regional differences in style and technique. Various bowls, stamp seals and beads of fine and even semi-precious stones are mainly from the north of the country, probably dating from the very end of the period. Pottery jars used for burial have also been found: the first coffins (16, No. 1).

(15) Seated cult figurine, H. Minha, 6th mill.

Chalcolithic Period

(4,000 — 3,150 BCE)

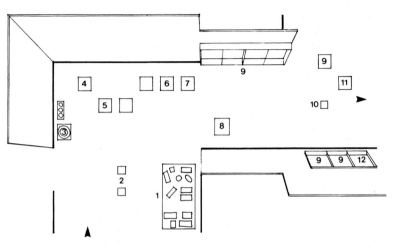

Room 302 focuses on the fourth millennium BCE when, a step closer to history, man first learned to smelt and work metals. Soon he was fashioning copper into tools and weapons, though stone long continued to be used for most implements. This transitional phase is denoted Chalcolithic — from the Greek words *chalcos* and *lithos*, meaning "copper" and "stone". Until recently, archaeologists were only vaguely familiar with this period, but research has now shown it to have had a highly developed culture of its own throughout Israel, including the outlying Negev, Judean desert and Golan regions. Its economy was based on agriculture and herding. Trade was gradually increasing, and in crafts a high level of artistic and technical ability was attained. Settlement was generally in villages but, toward the end of the period, most of these settlements were abandoned, leaving the outlying areas desolate and unoccupied for centuries to come.

In this period we also see a new attitude toward death and afterlife as reflected in funerary customs. At some sites, burial is seen to be in two phases: after initial burial (or possibly exposure), the bare bones were gathered and deposited in a special, small coffin — an ossuary (1). The pottery ossuaries on display, all found in a single cave not far from Tel Aviv, are mostly in the form of houses or huts, though some are of animal form.

An outstanding feature of the Chalcolithic period is its art. At Gilat, a large site in the northwestern Negev, a structure has come to light containing numerous interesting finds; two of the cult vessels there are pottery jars (2), one in the form of a ram bearing three jars on its back, and the other in the form of a seated nude woman (probably a fertility goddess), holding a large churn on her head. An actual pottery churn of this type can be seen in case (7), opposite.

The versatility of the Chalcolithic potters can also be

(1) Ossuaries, end of 4th mill.

seen in the huge, 1.4-meter high storage jar (3) from the Jordan valley, and from the other adjacent vessels. The parallel use of copper and stone in various tools and weapons is well demonstrated in cases (4).

The fine male and female statuettes (5) from Beer-sheba, carved in ivory, are delightful stylizations — probably relating to a fertility cult. Several objects in stone are indicative of commerce in this period (6): the

unusually large core of obsidian (volcanic glass), from which various blades could be chipped off, must have come from Anatolia; the obsidian mirror too may have been imported; and the basalt utensils were probably brought from northern Israel.

Continuing toward the next gallery, one comes to a model and photographs (8) of the Chalcolithic sanctuary discovered at Ein Gedi on the western shore of the

*ft, right: ivory statuettes, Beersheba, end of 4th mill.
iddle: cult vessel, Gilat, end of 4th mill.

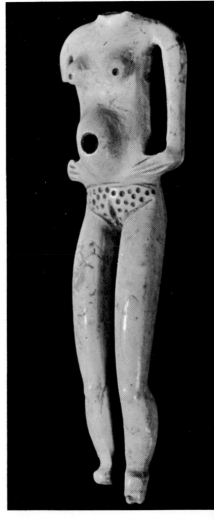

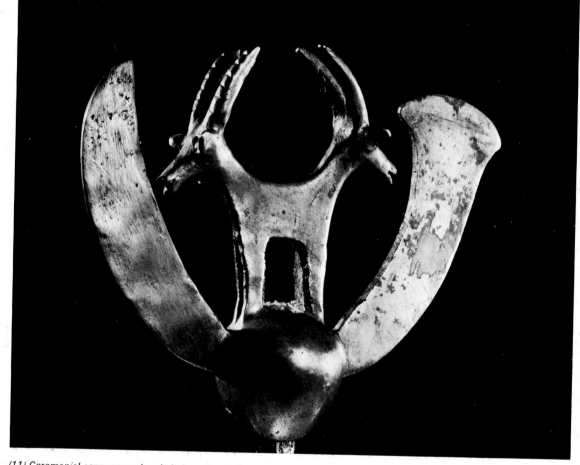

(11) Ceremonial copper macehead, Judean Desert Caves, end of 4th mill.

Dead Sea, where a ritual involving animal sacrifices was practiced. Opposite, in the wall-cases is one of the most extraordinary archaeological discoveries ever made in Israel (9): a hoard of 416 metal objects, seven stone weapons and six ivory articles, all found in 1961 wrapped in fiber mats in a cave in the Judean desert. The metal pieces include axes and chisels, hammers, "horns", "crowns", pots, "scepters" and 240 mace-heads of various shapes. The use of many of these objects is still unclear, but several of them are of outstanding beauty, such as the ibex scepter (10) and the splendid crown (11) with birds and ornamental gateways on its rim. In case (12) are various tools, linen cloth, a beaded purse and remains of foodstuffs: olive pits, grain, acorns and date pits, some found in another cave in the Judean desert.

Canaanite Age

(3,150 — 1,200 BCE)

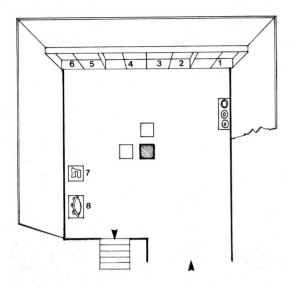

The Canaanite Age saw the rise of the major early civilizations throughout the ancient Near East. In Israel, this two-thousand year period witnessed the earliest urbanization, successive waves of foreign peoples, and the rise of the petty kingdoms of the Canaanite civilization as later reflected in the Bible.

The Early Canaanite Age

(3,150 —2,200 BCE)

The earliest settlements of the Early Canaanite Age were small and unwalled, and most of the finds are from tombs — pottery and stone vessels, ornaments, copper weapons and animal figurines (1). The early Canaanite economy which these finds reflect was based on agriculture and trade, with some industries including the metal crafts. The hoard of large bronze

(2) Spearheads, Kfar Monash, 3rd mill.

weapons and tools (2) may have been imported, and Egyptian influence can certainly be detected, reflecting close ties with Egypt. Several Egyptian jars (3) have been found in the south, some bearing the name of Narmer, the ruler who apparently united all Egypt into a single kingdom. Canaanite jars (3) have also been found in royal tombs in Egypt. Sporadic finds of cult objects, such as the stele from Arad (4), provide a glimpse into the realm of religion, as does the adjacent pottery model of a typical house of this period, also from Arad (it may represent a temple). Little local representational art has survived from this period and the fine ivory bull's head (5), from Beth Yerah on the Sea of Galilee may originally have been inlaid and may well have been imported, for it is close in style to similar Mesopotamian objects.

Late in the period, a new type of pottery, still hand-made, was introduced (6) — the polished red-and-black Khirbet Kerak ware, related to pottery from Syria, Anatolia and the Caucasus; it apparently points to the advent of foreign ethnic elements coming from the north. (Khirbet Kerak is the Arabic name of Beth Yerah where such pottery was first found in Israel.)

Around 3,000 BCE an intense process of urbanization set in, as seen at such outstanding sites as Megiddo, Beth Yerah (7) and Arad in the Negev (8). About four centuries later, many of the early cities were destroyed or had dwindled in size, and toward the end of the period further waves of migrants were to change the face of the entire ancient Near East.

Above: (5) Ivory bull's head, Beth Yerah, 3rd mill.
Below: (3) Egyptian jar fragment with name of King Narmer, Arad, 3rd mill.

The Middle Canaanite Age I
(2,200 — 2,000 BCE)

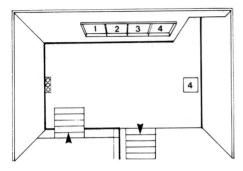

The final centuries of the third millennium BCE, denoted the Middle Canaanite Age I, are poorer in archaeological evidence. The earlier cities were deserted, and the smaller settlements now appearing were situated mostly in outlying areas. This, too, must have been a period of migration and unrest, and most of the surviving artificats are from tombs scattered about the countryside.

Typical of the pottery of this early phase is the shape which we today call "teapot" (1). In most of the tombs, the deceased was found buried together with his personal weapons and ornaments — especially daggers and spears (2). The ingots of copper and the other objects in case (3), found at a central Negev site, are indicative of trade and industry in this period.

A tomb to the north of Jerusalem was discovered containing many objects of this period, including a unique silver cup (4) embossed with various figures. In the drawing of the vessel, below, we see on the right a face within a rosette, held by two flanking figures (only one is preserved), while on the left is a double-faced, doubled-bodied creature apparently warding off flanking serpents. This seems to depict a mythological

(4) Silver cup, Ain Samiya 2250-2000 BCE.

scene of North Syrian or Mesopotamian origin.

At this point, the visitor can either turn right and descend the steps to the Middle Canaanite Age II display (see p. 108), or turn left and enter the Meyerhoff Glass Pavilion. It is recommended that the glass pavilion be visited first and then, returning to this same spot, the tour be resumed in historical sequence.

Ancient Glass

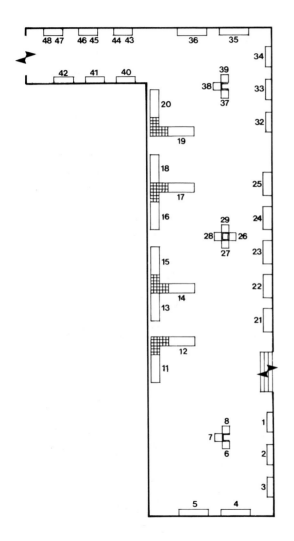

The nucleus of the glass display housed in the Joseph and Rebecca Meyerhoff Building is the collection donated by the late Eliahu Dobkin, one of the founders of the Israel Museum. (Note that the numbers referred to below correspond to those actually appearing on the display cases in the glass pavilion.)

Colored glass has been used to make vessels and other objects for over 3,500 years. Early in its history (1-3) it was often intended to imitate semi-precious stones and gems (3, No. 25), and was used in inlays on statues (3, No. 3) and in jewelry (3, No. 9). The early glass vessels, made by coating glass over a disposable core of sand or clay, were produced mainly in Mesopotamia and Egypt; later, production spread throughout the ancient Near East.

During the first millennium BCE, new centers of glass production arose, where small, multi-colored vessels were made in the shapes of classical pottery and metalware (4). This glass was traded in large quantities throughout the areas frequented by Phoenician and Greek seafarers and merchants. Later in this period, transparent, almost colorless glass was molded into utensils which were then engraved and polished

In Hellenistic times (3rd-1st centuries BCE), magnificent luxury vessels were produced, especially at Alexandria in Egypt. New techniques were developed, principally mosaic glass, in which motifs were built up of pieces of differently colored glass, which were subsequently fused together by heat to form a uniform multi-colored pattern *(millefiori)* (5, Nos. 8-17). This latter technique was used in making minute faces on beads (5, No. 27) and the fine Bacchus face on the pieces for inlay (5, No. 25).

During the mid 1st century BCE, the technique of blowing vessels from molten glass was first discovered and developed apparently in the region of Israel, for some

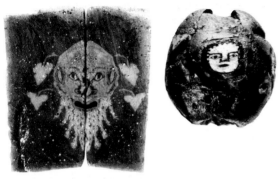

(5) Millefiori bead and inlay, Hellenistic period.

were in use. In the Byzantine period mold-blowing was used to make vessels with specifically Christian or specifically Jewish motifs (19, Nos. 6-9, 12-23). The unusually large plate (19, No. 1), from the Jewish cemetery at Beth Shearim near Haifa, bears an incised arcade design.

On the wall opposite these cases are several groups of finds from tombs of the Roman-Byzantine period (21-25), showing how glass vessels were an integral part of daily life at that time. Note the especially graceful forms of the tall jugs in case (25), on the left.

(4) Multi-colored glass vessel, Hellenistic period.

of the earliest dated finds of blown glass are from recent excavations in Jerusalem. This country, and the Phoenician coast to the north, remained a center of glass production for the next seven centuries.

Glass-blowing grew to become a mass-production industry, to meet the increasing demand for light, convenient vessels. The versatility of this technique led to the making of luxury wares (11-12), in addition to everyday vessels (13-14). Throughout the Roman world, glass soon replaced pottery for many household items, and even for such objects as cremation urns (13, No. 22). Ornament soon became an important feature, and the hot glass was molded (12), trailed (15), pinched (16) and impressed (29). Cold glass was occasionally cut or ground (26). The beauty of most of these vessels, however, is essentially derived from their fine flowing forms rather than from their ornamentation. The glistening, silvery sheen seen on some blown glass is the result of weathering over the centuries; this patina was entirely absent in antiquity.

The blowing of glass into molds was already perfected during Roman times (17), though other techniques

With the rise of Islam, Muslim glassworkers continued Byzantine techniques and forms, but they also introduced new methods and shapes (32-33). Former styles were revived, such as the wavy patterns encircling vessels.

Small case (37) contains two very rare Jewish "gold glasses" from Byzantine times (only eleven Jewish examples are known to exist). These are bowl bases with gold-leaf and painted ornamentation sandwiched between two layers of clear glass. They depict typically

Left: (12) Mold-blown vessel, Roman period.
Above: (19) Jewish glass vessel, Byzantine period.

Jewish symbols (including the *menorah*), which can also be seen in mosaics and on lamps of this period. Many similar pieces have been found in the catacombs of Rome, bearing Christian motifs, and the Jewish ones are apparently from this same source.

Cases (35-36) and (40-48) contain various temporary exhibits of glass, some of recent periods.

From here it is possible to enter room 312, devoted to the Roman period. It is recommended, however, that the visitor return to the entrance of the glass pavilion and resume the tour in its proper historical sequence.

Two Jewish "gold glasses", Rome, 4th cent. CE.

The Middle Canaanite Age II

(2,000 — 1,500 BCE)

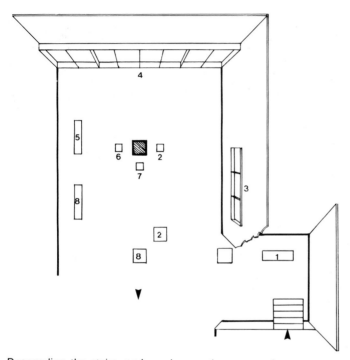

Descending the stairs, and passing another group of tomb finds (1), one enters the Middle Canaanite Age II display. This period, which spanned the first half of the second millennium BCE, saw the resettlement of Canaan. The major cities were re-established, and order and prosperity were restored. In biblical terms, this was the period of the Patriarchs, though no direct archaeological evidence for the patriarchal tradition has yet come to light. Canaanite material culture now reached its peak, stimulated by contacts with Egypt, Syria and Mesopotamia. Such contacts were mutual and Tel el-Yahudiyeh type pottery (2), with its dotted ornamentation, made its way from Canaan to Egypt, Syria and Cyprus. Note No. 1, depicting two bulls, a deer and a hunter with bow and arrow.

Documents now first appear locally, written in Akkadian in the cuneiform script (3), and individuals often possessed their own private seals — in Egyptian-style scarab form or cylindrical, in the Mesopotamian fashion.

Pottery (4), often painted and highly burnished, betrays Anatolian influences. Such forms as the angled bowls are found in both pottery and bronze.

(2) Tell el-Yahudiyeh vessel, first half 2nd mill.

The variety of objects found in a single Middle Canaanite Age II tomb, is well exemplified by the finds from Tel Nagila in the northern Negev (5): faience and alabaster vessels (Nos. 2-6), a fine bull-shaped vessel for liquids (No. 12), bone inlay pieces (No. 13), ostrich eggs (apparently used as bottles) (Nos. 15-16), seals (Nos. 18-20), pins and a dagger (Nos. 21-22).
A splendid jar (6), of the fine proportions and shape typical of this period, has a snake ornamentation on its handle.

Gold (7) has remained an extreme luxury throughout history, and it was usually reserved for cultic use or personal ornament. The small figurines of Canaanite gods, and the adjacent jewelry, were found together at Gezer, a large site between Jerusalem and Tel Aviv.

(8) Offering vessel and mold of Astarte figurine (with modern casting) Nahariya, first half 2nd mill.

In a sanctuary discovered at Nahariya, on the northern coast of Israel, numerous cult objects have come to light (8): seven-cup offering vessels (No. 1), a mould for a statuette of a goddess (No. 2; the casting is modern), small silver figurines (No. 3), a juglet with a crouching monkey on its neck, holding a hand over his eyes (No. 5), and beads in the form of a bird and a lion (Nos. 7-8).

During the course of the Middle Canaanite Age II, a period of decided prosperity, the larger settlements came to be fortified with massive walls and moats, as renewed pressure was again felt from northern invaders, who moved through Canaan and overran Egypt. These were the Hyksos, ethnically mixed hordes made up of Hurrians, Hittites and other nations, who overthrew the Egyptian Middle Kingdom. They, in turn, were eventually overcome by the rising 18th dynasty of Egypt, a development which ushered in the New Kingdom there, as well as the Late Canaanite Age in this country.

The Late Canaanite Age
(1,500—1,200 BCE)

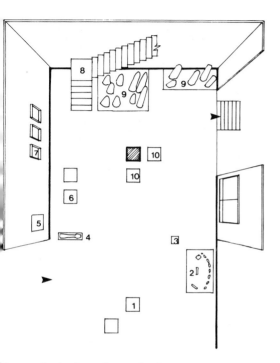

(3) Pottery mask, Hazor, 14th-13th cents. BCE.

Canaan in the Late Canaanite Age was dominated by the Egypt of the New Kingdom. Though Egyptian impact is felt in almost every cultural sphere, the influence of northern Syria and the Hittite empire in eastern Anatolia is also quite evident. Akkadian became the *lingua franca* of the entire region, and a complete archive of letters (discovered at el-Amarna in Egypt), written in cuneiform and sent by various Canaanite rulers to their Egyptian overlord, has revealed the intricacies and intrigues of local and international politics in this period.

Outstanding pottery of the Late Canaanite Age can be seen in the form of (1) large, open jars (kraters) ornamented with birds, bulls, rams and dolphins, painted in red and black — pottery known as Bichrome Ware.

The major cities of Canaan continued to flourish in splendor. One of the largest centers in the north was Hazor, where several temples have been uncovered. A shrine there (2) contained a series of small basalt steles, one of which bears a sacred symbol. Several stone and metal figurines, as well as cult masks (3), were also found on the site. Looking at the two sides of one of the masks, one can see how painstakingly pottery restorers work to piece together the past.

Crossing the hall, the visitor comes to the majestic lion *orthostat* (4) which flanked the entrance to another of the temples at Hazor. This stone clearly indicates North Syrian-Hittite stylistic influence. On the wall behind the lion is a model of the temple from which it comes (5).

A magnificent example of the pottery imported into Canaan from the west is a Mycenean krater (6), found in a tomb at Laish (Dan), at the northern tip of Israel. It is painted with a chariot scene running all around it. Other imported objects include a sickle-sword (7), probably bent at the death of its warrior-owner.

Ascending the stairs (8) to the Braumüller Gallery, one enters the world of Late Canaanite cult and religion, displaying various statuettes and figurines of deities in gold, silver and bronze. Adjacent to the central pillar is a basalt relief depicting lions, from a Late Canaanite temple at Beth-Shean. At the far end of the gallery is a model of a Canaanite temple at Lachish, and many of the finer objects discovered in it are shown in the display cases here. Another case contains a selection of scarabs and seals from various sites.

(8) The Braumüller Gallery.

(2) Shrine of the Stelae, 14th-13th cents. BCE.

A major archaeological find in recent years came to light in a cemetery at Deir el-Balah, south of Gaza. There were numerous large pottery coffins (9), the lids of which are in the form of the upper torso and head of the deceased, rendered in a crude "Egyptian" style. The outstanding example at the far left bears a rather vivid portrait. The objects (10) found together with and inside these coffins include a rich array of jewelry in gold and semi-precious stones, scarab seals, mirrors, implements and utensils of bronze and some pottery. Many of these objects, some of them very minute and finely made, were imported from Egypt, Cyprus and Mycenean Greece.

The major sources of imported pottery in this period were Egypt, Mycenean Greece, Cyprus and Syria, and some of these vessels are most graceful (11). The bronze mirror found at Acre on Israel's northern coast (12), with a handle in the form of a nude female, is probably from Egypt.

Toward the end of this period, both internal stability and external Egyptian control slackened, and the land of Canaan was vulnerable to invasion. Foreign elements again began penetrating, this time the Philistines and other Sea-Peoples coming from the Mediterranean, and the Israelites coming from the desert. These events heralded the Israelite period.

(8) Model of Fosse Temple, Lachish, 13th cent. BCE.

(12) Bronze mirror, Acre, 14th cent. BCE.

(6) Mycenean chariot vase, Tel Dan, 14th cent. BCE.

Israelite Period
(1,200-586 BCE)

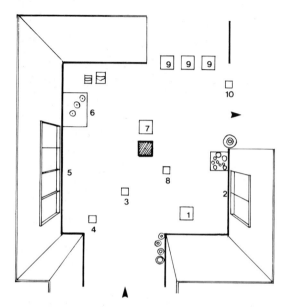

(3) Philistine figurine, Ashdod, 12th cent. BCE.

The Early Israelite Period
(1,200 — 1,000 BCE)

The settlement of the Israelite tribes in Canaan, the establishment of an Israelite kingdom, its rise and eventual fall, span the Israelite period. This period is also denoted the Iron Age, for it was at this time that iron began to oust bronze as the dominant metal for tools and weapons. Upon entering the hall, to the right, are several iron implements and objects used in early iron-making (1).

This phase corresponds with the period of the settlement of the Israelite tribes in Canaan, following the Exodus from Egypt, and the days of Joshua and the Judges. The Israelites sought to settle the Galilee, the

central hill-country (Judea and Samaria) and the northern Negev, introducing new types of pottery into these regions (2), alongside older Canaanite forms.

At much the same time that the Israelites were penetrating the interior of Canaan, the Philistines and other Sea-Peoples were gaining a foothold along the southern and central coasts; these peoples had spread out from the north of the Aegean Sea, fanning over much of the eastern Mediterranean basin including Israel's coast. Across the hall are typical examples of the Philistine material culture: a goddess-and-chair figurine from Ashdod (3), nicknamed "Ashdoda", and a finely painted beer-jug with drinking spout (4). The colorful Philistine pottery and other objects (5) are highlighted by the lion-headed rhyton (drinking-horn) on the upper

(7) Cult vessel, Sa'asa, 12th cent. BCE.

tier in the third case. A series of Philistine temples was uncovered at Tell Qasile in northern Tel Aviv, and the cult stands (6) found there show something of the rituals practiced, as do the vessels (7) used for libation or possibly ritual drinking.

The Israelites and the Philistines both found a relative political vacuum in Canaan at the time of their arrival, for the Egyptian empire, which had encompassed Canaan till now, was in its final decline, as were other of the major empires of this period. Though the invaders destroyed many Canaanite centers, there still remained Canaanite enclaves in the northern valleys and along the coastal plain, where the older Canaanite religion continued to be practiced, as is reflected in the bronze bull (8) and in the cult stands (9) from Beth-Shean and Taanach, bearing scenes with snakes, lions, cherubs and sphinxes. These stands were probably used for burning incense. The fine stand from Ashdod (10) bears a small orchestra of musicians playing the flute, a tambourine and the pipes. These indications of Canaanite cultic music bring to mind the ritual music and psalms later sung in Solomon's temple.

117

Philistine "beer-jug", Tell 'Aitun, 12th cent. BCE.

(10) Cult stand, Ashdod, 10th cent. BCE.

(9) Cult stand, Taanach, 10th cent. BCE.

The Late Israelite Period
(1,000—586 BCE)

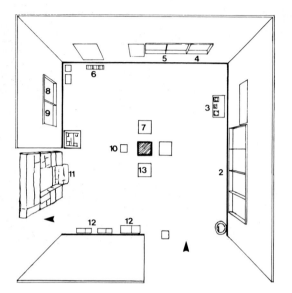

This phase began with the consolidation of the Israelites under King David, and the rise of his empire. The formerly nomadic Israelites had absorbed much of the culture of their new surroundings, as can be seen in the objects of their daily life: the huge storage jar from Dan (1) and various household bronze and pottery utensils (2). The rougher, hand-made pottery in the left-hand case is typical of such Negev sites as Kadesh-Barnea, a major Israelite fortress on the edge of Sinai.

The horned altars from Megiddo (3) vividly illustrate the biblical institution of seeking refuge at an altar by seizing its horns.

David made Jerusalem his capital, and his son Solomon forged it into the national and religious center of the Israelite people — a status it has retained ever since. These kings allied themselves with the Phoenicians, who lived in Lebanon. The influence of this neighboring nation is strongly felt in many of the objects on display, for example in the beautiful carved

(6) Stone balustrade, Ramat Rahel, 9th-7th cents. BCE.

(5) Carved ivory, Samaria, 9th cent. BCE.

ivories (4-5) discovered in the royal palace at Samaria, capital of the northern kingdom of Israel. Most of the ivories are in Phoenician style, which was greatly influenced by Egyptian art, but some of the motifs here are to be found throughout the ancient Near East: the lion mauling a bull (5, top right), the sphinx (5, lower left), the "woman in the window" (5, upper right), the palmettes and many others. Most of these ivories had been inlaid in wooden furniture. The "woman in the window" motif shows a stone balustrade identical to that from Ramat Rahel (6), the site of a royal Judean palace-fortress just south of Jerusalem.

The Phoenicians were major seafaring traders in this period, and the amulets and other ornaments found in their cemetery at Akhziv on the northern coast (7) are indicative of the extent of trade with Egypt, though some of these pieces may have been made locally. The fine quality of Phoenician pottery, a stock item of their trade throughout the Mediterranean Sea, is also well demonstrated here (8-9); that Phoenician fertility figurines, such as that in case (9) on the middle tier, were exported also, is known from an entire cargo of similar figurines from a shipwreck of this period found off the Akhziv coast.

David and Solomon built cities throughout Israel, and the largest one in the north was at Hazor, the former Canaanite center, where carved bone objects (10) have come to light. Hazor and other sites have revealed a truly Israelite style of architecture. This style persisted even after Solomon's empire split into the twin kingdoms of Judah in the south and Israel in the north. The fates of these two states remained closely linked, and both were usually subservient to one or other of the major powers of the day. In the north, the kings of Israel

(3) Astarte figurines, from Judean sites, 8th-6th cents. BCE.

continued to fortify and rebuild Hazor (11), and it is here that we see a most outstanding and typical feature of royal Israelite architecture — the Proto-Ionic capital as archaeologists sometimes call it — used in an entry-way built by King Ahab. Such capitals have been found at Megiddo and Samaria as well, and also in Judah (12) at Gezer, Ramat Rahel and Jerusalem.

Recent excavations in Jerusalem have yielded many interesting objects from the Israelite period, and for the first time it is possible to construct a relatively accurate picture of life in the city some 2,700 years ago. One of the more charming finds is an Astarte statuette (13, upper center) the type of household figurine denounced by the Hebrew prophets in the Bible.

Left: (9) Phoenician figurine, Akhziv, 8th-6th cents. BCE.
Above: (8) Pomegranate bowl, Lahav, 8th-7th cents. BCE.
Below: (9) "Akhziv" jugs, Akhziv, 8th-6th cents. BCE

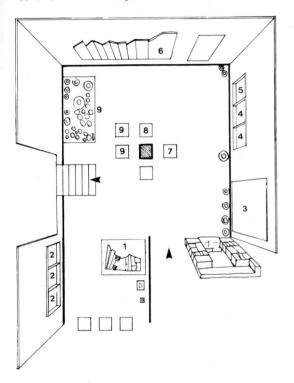

Passing the Hazor entryway one turns to the left and encounters the holy-of-holies (1) from the Israelite sanctuary at Arad in the Negev. The royal fortress and administrative center at Arad, on the frontier with hostile Edom, was first built during the 10th century BCE and was destroyed and rebuilt several times before its final destruction in the 6th century BCE. About one eighth of the fortress was occupied by the sanctuary, which contained the same basic rooms as Solomon's temple in Jerusalem: an outer court, a porch, a main hall and a holy-of-holies; all flanked by rows of service rooms. In the outer court there was a large altar for burnt offerings. In the porch, flanking the entrance to the main hall, there were two flat stone bases for columns — comparable to the twin columns in the Jerusalem temple. The raised holy-of-holies (1) contains two incense altars, still bearing traces of burnt matter, a stone stele and a platform. Since nothing whatsoever remains of Solomon's temple, this is the closest we have come to seeing what it was like — though it was certainly much more splendid than this mere frontier-town chapel.

In the cases opposite the Arad shrine are various objects (2) from the sanctuary, including several inscribed potsherds (ostraca).

Crossing once again past the Hazor entryway, there is a large photograph (3) on the wall showing another specifically Israelite architectural feature, the "four-room house" — found in almost every Israelite town excavated in this country. Household vessels and other objects (4) reflect daily life in these Israelite cities. Lachish, the second city of Judah, was twice taken by siege, once in 701 BCE and then, finally, in 586 BCE, by the Babylonians under Nebuchadnezzar. The arrowheads and catapult stones shown in case (5) are from the earlier siege. On the wall to the left (6) is a depiction of the capture of Lachish in 701 BCE by Sennacherib, King of Assyria (the plaster cast of a relief from his palace). On the left is the storming of the ramparts, while on the right the Judean townsfolk are being taken into exile. The Assyrians often erected monumental steles to commemorate their victories, and several fragments of such steles (7) are shown, along with a clay prism recording Sennacherib's Judean campaign, including the siege of Jerusalem and the capture of many towns.

(1) Holy-of-Holies, Israelite sanctuary at Arad.

Left: (7) Assyrian prism of Sennacherib, 691 BCE.
Above: (8) Assyrian-type bowl, Tell el-Qitaf, 8th cent. BCE.

Various Assyrian vessels (8), generally of fine work-manship, have been found in Israel; note, on the upper shelf, the marble bowl with duck's-head and bull's-feet supports, and the magnificent lobed bronze bowl on the lower shelf.

Recent excavations have revealed much evidence of Jerusalem in Late Israelite times (9), presenting a cross-section of life in the capital city of Judah.

International political intrigue eventually brought about the destruction of the Kingdom of Israel and its capital at Samaria, in 721 BCE. Judah, several times invaded by the Assyrians, thrived only until 586 BCE, when Nebuchadnezzar II of Babylonia conquered Jeru-salem and burned the temple built by Solomon some 350 years before. The Judeans, or Jews as they now came to be called, were exiled to Mesopotamia, and the Israelite nation entered a new and significantly formative stage in its history, especially in the spiritual realm.

Persian Period

(Late 6th cent. BCE — Late 4th cent. BCE)

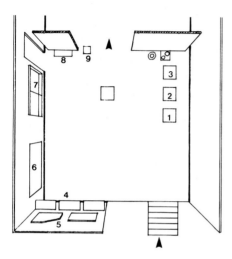

After ascending the stairs, continue straight on to case (1).

Only half a century after the catastrophe that caused the overthrow of the kingdom of Judah, the ancient Near East was conquered by the Achemenid dynasty of Persia. In 538 BCE, Judah became a minor province within the Persian Empire, and was now known as *Yehud*. Soon the Jews were permitted to return to their homeland and to rebuild the temple in Jerusalem. Under the leadership of Ezra and Nehemiah, in the 5th century BCE, the political, social and religious life of the Jews in Judea was reorganized and set on a firm national basis.

During this period, fine Greek painted pottery (1) was imported in large quantities, and Egyptian-style figurines and amulets enjoyed continued popularity. Glass vessels and beads had become commonplace, and the splendid craftsmanship of Achemenid Persia is exemplified here by the beautiful gold earring in the form of a goat's head (upper shelf, center) and the bronze censer with a duck's-head handle (lower shelf, right).

Pottery figurines and small incense altars (2) were used in local sanctuaries and in private homes; Egyptian influence, felt for so long in Israel, was now largely replaced by Greek, Phoenician and Persian stylistic trends.

A town of this period was excavated at Tel Megadim on the coast south of Haifa; the finds from this site (3) reflect the daily life and occupations of its inhabitants.

(1) Bronze censer, Khirbet Ibsan, Persian period.

Hebrew Script and Inscriptions

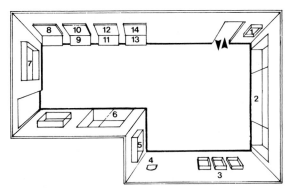

(7) Ostracon, Mesad Hashavyahu, 7th cent. BCE.

Crossing to case (4), one finds coins inscribed *Yehud* in Hebrew script — the name of the Persian province of Judea. This name also appears on official stamps on jar-handles. On the wall above, to the right (5), is an inscription from a burial cave in the Judean Hills; the word on the left reads: "Jerusalem", and this 6th century BCE inscription, from the days before the destruction of Solomon's temple, is the earliest mention we know of the Holy City in Hebrew, outside the Bible.

The chart of letters (6) shows the development of the ancient Hebrew alphabet, from the second millennium BCE on, and how the Greek, Latin and Arabic alphabets evolved from it. Case (7) displays a cross-section of the development of ancient Hebrew script, and demonstrates the diversity of materials and objects inscribed.

Turning to the left, one enters the Hecht Pavilion of Hebrew Script and Inscriptions. Soon after the first appearance of alphabetic script 3,500 years ago — a major contribution to western civilization — the Canaanites and Israelites developed a 22-letter alphabet written from right to left, with the letters named and learned by rote in a fixed order which has

varied little over the centuries and is reflected to a great extent in the order of the English alphabet.

To the Jewish people, writing and script have always been considered sacred, and the Jews have aptly been called the People of the Book. The Israelites utilized writing in their everyday life, in ritual, in commerce and in art. A beautiful seal (1) exemplifies all three of these aspects, for the lyre was an instrument used in the Jerusalem temple, the seal itself was used in signing documents of commerce, and the design on the seal is a masterpiece of stone engraving.

Case (2) displays the varieties of uses of script in Israelite times. In (3) are inscriptions concerning trade and commerce, on various weights and measures. The Siloam Inscription (4; plaster copy) records the hewing

(6) Inscribed vessels, Kuntillet Ajrud, 8th cent. BCE.

of King Hezekiah's water tunnel in Jerusalem, a feat also mentioned in the Bible.

The "House of God" noted in a 6th century BCE ostracon from Arad (5) probably refers to the temple in Jerusalem; and seal impressions of King Alexander Janneus (5) mention his title as high priest (1st century BCE). Jars bearing the Hebrew word for "holy" had held sacrifices, which were forbidden for profane use and thus specially marked.

Near the border between Israel and the Sinai peninsula, archaeologists have recently discovered an Israel-ite fortress-shine, on the pilgrims' road to Mount Sinai, unique in the number and type of Hebrew inscriptions found (6). The large stone basin bears a dedication to Yahu, God of the Hebrews, who is also mentioned in a large inscription written in ink on plaster. The inscribed pottery jars also bear depictions of human and semi-divine figures as well as animals.

In room 310 one saw the Lachish relief and the Arad sanctuary. The ostraca (7) from these two sites are official administrative and military reports. The long

Opp: Group of seals and bullae 8th-6th cents. BCE.

letter from Mesad Hashavyahu (7), on the coast south of Tel Aviv, is a peasant's appeal to the authorities concerning a wrong done to him by his employer. These documents are from the last fifty years of the kingdom of Judah. In the adjacent case is the only known Hebrew papyrus surviving from the Israelite period — though there is clear evidence that this early "paper" was often used.

In antiquity, a person's seal was his signature. Amongst the Phoenicians (8), Arameans (8), Ammonites (9), Moabites (9) and Hebrews (11), the general shape of the seal is uniform, but differences are found in the motifs employed, in the forms of the letters and, especially, in the names of the owners. Often the style of the script can indicate the date of a seal, at least approximately.

Most of the Hebrew or Israelite seals are distinguished by their total lack of ornamentation, in keeping with the biblical law against graven images. Note especially the women's seal (10) and the masterpiece from Megiddo (12, upper left) bearing a crowned griffin and the name Haman. Royal officials in Judah noted their titles on their seals (13), and one example also bears a striking depiction of a fighting cock (14, middle right). Jar handles (15) bearing official Judean stamps, inscribed "Belonging to the King", have been found on many sites throughout southern Israel.

Once again entering room 311A, we see on the left two inscriptions of historical importance: a sign (8) carved in stone, showing the way "To the place of trumpeting...", from Herod's temple in Jerusalem; and a plaque (9) marking the site of the reburial of the bones of King Uzziah. These two inscriptions, both from the later period of the second temple, lead one into the display of objects from Hellenistic times.

Left: (14) Hebrew seal impression, 8th-7th cents. BCE.
Right: (10) Seal of Jezebel 9th-8th cents. BCE.
Below: (9) Uzziah's burial plaque, Jerusalem, 1st cent. BCE.

135

Hellenistic, Roman and Byzantine Periods

(Late 4th century BCE — Early 7th Century CE)

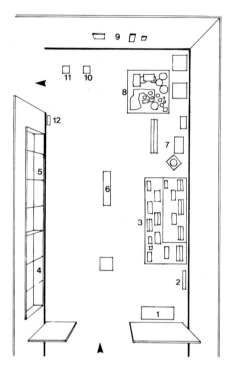

The Hellenistic Period

(Late 4th century — late 1st century BCE)

In the wake of the conquest of the east by Alexander the Great, late in the 4th century BCE, the Near East was exposed to increasing cultural influences from the west, leading to a new, blended culture collectively known as Hellenism. Around 165 BCE, the Jews were able to throw off the yoke of the Hellenistic kings of Syria, the Seleucids, and Jewish independence was restored. The new dynasty, the Maccabeans or Hasmoneans, ruled until 37 BCE when they were ousted by Herod the Great. It was under Herod and his successors that local architecture and art reached their zenith, 2,000 years ago. For Christianity this period is of great significance, for it included the lifetime of Jesus; indeed, the objects in this gallery, as well as those in the Shrine of the Book (see p. 2), provide the

This epoch in the history of the land of Israel is symbolized by the second temple in Jerusalem, by the Mishnah and the Talmud. It was a crucial phase in the intellectual, religious and national development of the Jewish people.

(2) Aramaic burial inscription, Jerusalem, 1st cents. BCE-CE.

material backdrop for the Gospels, and for the events so vividly described in the books of the Jewish historian Flavius Josephus.

The Jews have always placed great importance on their burial customs. The well-preserved wooden coffin with bone and wood inlays (1), found together with the other objects in caves near Ein Gedi on the western shore of the Dead Sea, is a rare surviving example of what must have been a common form of burial in the 1st century BCE.

Burial in Jerusalem, the Holy City, has always been considered particularly desirable, for, according to a Jewish belief, those buried there shall be the first to rise upon the coming of the Messiah. The tomb inscription (2) from northern Jerusalem, written in archaic Hebrew script, mentions a Jerusalemite who died in Mesopotamia and whose remains had been brought back to the city for burial.

Right: (12) Pontius Pilate inscription, Caesarea, 26-36 CE.
Below: (7) Jewish sarcophagus, Jerusalem, 1st cent. BCE.

137

The large group of ossuaries (3) from the Jerusalem region reveal the custom of two-stage burials: initially the body was laid out in a family burial cave; a year or so later, the remaining bones would be placed in a special chest or ossuary, subsequently stored in the tomb. Some of these boxes bear inscriptions naming the deceased.

Crossing the room to case (4), we see some of the fine pottery of the Hellenistic period, from a site in northern Israel. Adjacent case (5) contains later material — from Masada, the desert fortress. The Roman conquest of Judea, and the ensuing Jewish revolt in 66—70 CE, resulted in the destruction of Judea as an autonomous state. The last diehard insurgents were trapped at Masada and, on the very brink of slaughter by the Roman legions, they collectively took their own lives, in 73 CE.

Three years earlier the Romans had laid siege to Jerusalem. Eventually, the temple was burned and the rest of the city was destroyed, quarter by quarter. Vivid evidence of this has come to light in excavations over the last fifteen years, especially in the Jewish Quarter of the Old City, where parts of a well-to-do neighborhood have come to light. The objects in case (6) are from the splendid mansions there, and most of the following exhibits in this room are from the same excavations. The upheaval resulting from the failure of this great Jewish revolt led Judaism toward a process of recrystallization. This culminated in the massive edifice of religion which guides the life of Jews to this day, focusing around the synagogue and founded upon the oral law — the Mishnah and the Talmud.

One of Jerusalem's outstanding features is its stonework, and the use of stone in art and architecture is long-established. Even today there is a municipal by-law requiring that façades of buildings be constructed

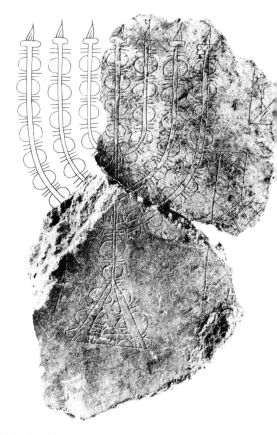

Right: (11) Menorah graffito, Jerusalem, 1st cent. BCE.

of stone, to preserve the outward unified appearance of the city. The beautifully carved Corinthian capital (7) is from the Jewish Quarter excavations, while the equally fine sarcophagus was found in a Jewish tomb on Mount Scopus.

Stone jars and tables (8) were another facet of Jerusalem's stoneworking industry in antiquity. Such jars are

138

(8) Stone vessels and tables, mosaics and (9) fresco fragments, Jerusalem, 1st cents. BCE-CE.

referred to in the story of the miracle at Cana, in the New Testament. The mosaics, similar to those in Herod's palaces at Masada, are among the earliest discovered in Israel.

The fragments of frescoes (9) from the Jewish Quarter excavations recall Roman wall-paintings found at Pompeii in Italy.

A unique find in the Jewish Quarter is a fragmentary glass jug (10) with moulded ornamentation; this vessel is signed by its maker — Ennion, a master craftsman known from several similar vessels.

The *menorah* (11), or seven-branched candlestick in the Jerusalem temple, was the foremost symbol of the Jews in antiquity, and as such it appears on Hasmonean coins (see p. 84) and on the Arch of Titus in Rome. In the ruins of a house in the Jewish quarter, some 250 meters away from the site of the temple, fragments of wall plaster were found bearing the incised pattern of the *menorah* — the earliest known detailed depiction of this symbol.

In excavations at Caesarea, the capital of Roman Palaestina, an inscription (12) came to light mentioning the name of Pontius Pilate. This is the only archaeological confirmation of the existence of this governor.

The Roman Period
(Late 1st—3rd centuries CE)

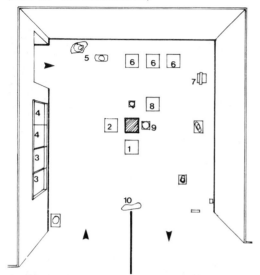

Above: (11) Marble griffin, Erez, 3rd cent. CE.
Below: (3) Bronze leopard, Avdat, 1st-2nd cents. CE.

Entering the Roman period, one is confronted by one of the few known bronze portraits of the Emperor Hadrian (1), discovered by chance south of Beth-Shean in 1975. This unique, slightly larger-than-life statue, although damaged, is the finest example of Roman portraiture ever found in Israel. Another fine piece of Roman metalwork is the beautiful iron parade helmet (2), also of the 2nd century CE; accompanying it are pieces of a Roman soldier's armor. They were found together in the vicinity of Jerusalem.

At this period the southern part of Israel, the Negev, was mostly controlled by the Nabateans. In case (3) are examples of typical Nabatean pottery, various small bronzes, some of them probably imported, and jewelry. Hidden in the large bronze jar was a hoard of 10,000 Roman silver coins found at Mampsis (Kurnub), some of which are displayed here.

These objects are typical of the Roman influence on

(7) Stone tomb-door, Jaffa, 3rd cent. CE.

(5) Artemis of Ephesus, Caesarea, 2nd-3rd cents. CE.

141

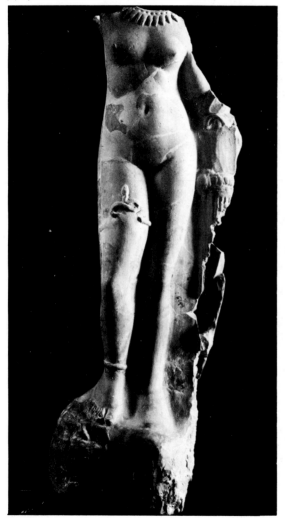

(6) Aphrodite, Mt. Carmel, 1st-2nd cents. CE.

local culture throughout the country. Hadrian sought to strengthen his influence, and founded a Roman city over the ruins of Jerusalem. In reaction to this and other of his measures, the Jews made a second attempt to regain independence from Rome, in 132 CE — the Bar Kokhba revolt. Most of the archaeological finds associated with this war are on display in the Shrine of the Book (see p. 2), but some of these remarkably preserved objects can be seen in cases (4).

Just beyond (4), the glass pavilion can be entered to the left (see p. 102). The visitor can continue on to two pieces of Roman sculpture (5) — *Artemis of Ephesus* and the *Satyr* from Caesarea, of the 2nd—3rd centuries CE. This latter city, founded by Herod the Great toward the end of the 1st century BCE, used by the Romans as the capital of Palaestina, is representative of the rise of the Roman cities in this country. Cases (6) contain various objects typical of the particularly local Roman way of life.

The adjacent fragment of a stone door from a tomb (7) found at Jaffa, near Tel Aviv, is carved in imitation of a wooden door, complete with metal studs and a panel containing the figure of an actor with his mask.

Roman control in Israel is further represented by bricks, tiles and coins (8) stamped with the mark of the Tenth Legion of the Roman army. They bear witness to the nearly two hundred year garrison of this force in Jerusalem. The column (9) bearing a Roman inscription from Caesarea and the monumental inscription (10) from the aqueduct of that city show further evidence of the Roman presence in Israel.

The sculptures along the wall (11) are typical of provincial towns throughout the Roman empire (from left to right): a god or hero, from Beth-Shean (1st century CE); a Maenad, also from Beth-Shean (late Roman); and a griffin, from Erez south of Ashkelon (3rd century CE).

(2) Iron parade helmet, Jerusalem hills, 2nd cent. CE.

The Late Roman and Byzantine Periods
(3rd—early 7th centuries CE)

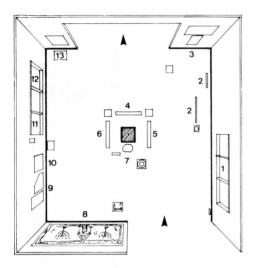

on its walls was a large dedicatory inscription (3) mentioning its builder.

A lead coffin (4) of the 3rd century CE bears clearly pagan motifs; a very similar lead coffin (5), which came to light in a 4th-century tomb in Jerusalem, bears Christian symbols, while a third lead coffin (6), from Beth Shearim and also of the 4th century CE, closely

(1) Byzantine pilgrim's flask, 6th cent. CE.

Early in the 4th century CE, with the rise of Christianity as the official religion of the Byzantine empire, the Holy Land and especially Jerusalem became important Christian focal points, with numerous scattered churches and monasteries. From this time on, Roman paganism declined and gradually disappeared. Christian pilgrims coming to the holy sites sought mementos of their journey, and they would often take home with them sacred water or oil in small flasks bearing Christian symbols and inscriptions, specially made for this purpose (1). In Byzantine churches, the altar was set off from the nave by marble chancel screens (2), most of which bore Christian symbols. One of the most magnificent Byzantine churches in Jerusalem was the Nea, or New Church of St. Mary, Mother of God, built by the Emperor Justinian around 540 CE. The recent excavations in the Jewish Quarter uncovered a huge cistern belonging to this church, and

(2) Marble chancel screen from Massuot Itshaq, and pillar from Khirbet Hkadat, Byzantine period.

resembles its counterparts but bears the *menorah* motif and is thus clearly Jewish. A similar phenomenon can be seen in the Jewish synagogues of the Late Roman and Byzantine periods, which were ornamented by the same craftsmen as contemporaneous Christian buildings, but with Jewish motifs instead of Christian symbols (7). The splendid synagogue floor mosaic from Beth-Shean (8), of the 6th century CE, depicts the curtained Ark of the Law which held the Torah scrolls. This is flanked by *menorahs* accompanied by the *shofar* (ram's horn) and an incense shovel. The general layout of the four columns and the arched ark can also be seen on the silver coins of the Bar Kokhba revolt, representing the temple in Jerusalem.

Many synagogue mosaics contain secular motifs, as those from Yafia (9). In most synagogues of this period there were inscriptions blessing the donors of the various rooms, mosaic floors, columns and the like; the inscription on plaster (10) is from the synagogue at Rehob, near Beth-Shean.

Case (11) shows the variegated applications of the *menorah* motif, the principal symbol of the Jewish people in antiquity.

The extensive Jewish cemetery at Beth-Shearim near Haifa has yielded many fascinating objects from Byzantine times (12), including fragmentary marble sarcophagi and tomb inscriptions in Hebrew, Aramaic and Greek.

In Samaritan houses, the *mezuzah* (doorpost scroll) was carved on the stone doorpost itself at the outer gate (13). One of the two examples on display here is from Shechem (Nablus), the Samaritan center.

(6) Jewish lead sarcophagus, Beth Shearim, 4th cent. CE.

Opp: Bronze head of Emperor Hadrian, 2nd cent. CE.

Oil lamp with Jewish symbols, Byzantine period.

Above right: (11) Jewish amulet, Roman -Byzantine period.
Right: (11) Jewish talisman, Roman-Byzantine period.
Below: (9) Synagogue mosaic, Yafia, 3rd-4th cents. CE.

Oil Lamps

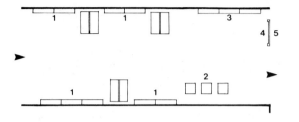

The core of the display in this gallery, devoted to the oil lamp in ancient Israel, is the Louis and Carmen Warschaw Collection donated by courtesy of the Fund for Higher Education in Israel in 1976. Oil lamps — which are of considerable interest to archaeologists — give evidence of regional stylistic variations. Some Jewish lamps bear motifs which appear to have had nationalistic associations and complement other finds in the study of ancient Jewish art, such as ossuaries and coins.

In the cases along the left-hand wall (1), the principal groups of oil lamps in Israel are shown according to period. The early lamps were open bowls with rims pinched to form a crude nozzle. In Hellenistic times, under Greek influence, this developed into a nozzle of tubular shape and the body became enclosed. The lamps of the Herodian period, made on the potter's wheel, were rather plain in contrast to those of the Roman period, which were mostly made in molds and often had decorative motifs and scenes. In the period between the destruction of the temple in Jerusalem (70 CE) and the Bar Kokhba revolt (132 CE), an ornamented type of oil lamp was made by the Jews remaining in Judea. In later Roman and Byzantine times, oil lamp ornamentation was less figurative, and we see the *menorah* design on Jewish lamps (see p. 145) and clearly Christian symbols on other examples. Muslim

(1) Herodian, late Roman and Byzantine lamps.

150

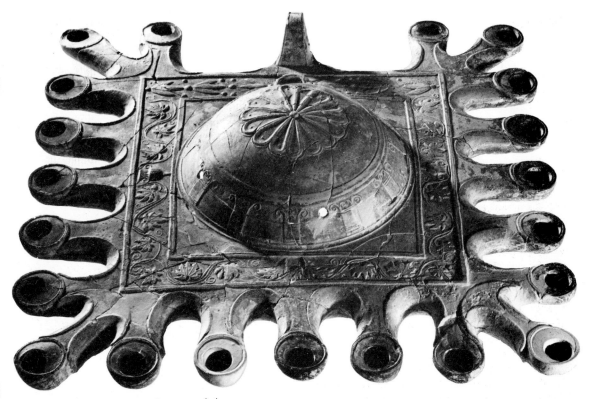

(2) Twenty-one nozzle oil lamp, Roman period.

oil lamps continued the Byzantine style, but there was also a return to much earlier, open types with folded rims forming the nozzle.

In the freestanding cases (2) there are various luxurious bronze and pottery lamps of the Roman-Byzantine period, ornamented with such motifs as the head of an elephant, that of a bull or a horse, or in the form of ships' prows; also to be seen are lamps intended to provide greater light: one for twenty-one wicks, a fine example of a Roman molded lamp, and a rather grotesque, over-ornate Byzantine lamp with nozzles on several levels. In Byzantine times, too, hanging lamps with glass oil containers were introduced (see p. 102), a further improvement in increasing the yield of light.

Many of the Roman-Byzantine tombs discovered in Israel contained jewelry, besides oil lamps and other personal objects. In the wall cases on the right (3) are objects found in the Christian lead coffin shown in room 313 (see p. 144), and gold jewelry from various other tombs of this period — including fine filigree earrings, carved gems and a ring engraved with the figure of a city-goddess.

The two mosaic fragments (4) are from an eleven-meter long portion of a floor found at Kisufim, south of Gaza. The mosaic pavement belonged to a 6th century CE church and the fragments shown here depict Alexander hunting, and a lioness with her cub.

A dozen kilometers to the north, at Or Haner between Ashkelon and Gaza, a painted tomb of the 4th century CE came to light, containing a row of portraits of the deceased. Two of the portraits (5) are shown here, reminiscent of Roman period mummy portraits in Egypt. Over the doorway of this tomb, which probably belonged to a pagan family, was the Greek inscription: "Enter! No one is immortal!"

(5) Tomb painting, Or Haner, 4th cent. CE.

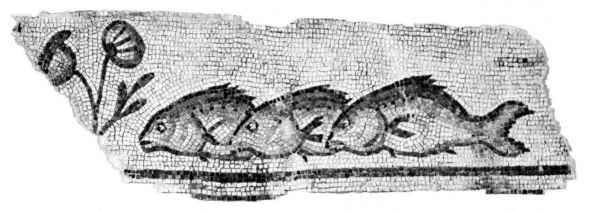

The city of Beth-Shean, south of the Sea of Galilee, was a major center in Roman-Byzantine times, and a large Jewish community flourished there alongside the Christian population. In the surrounding villages, too, there were many Jews, and the entire region is dotted with the ruins of ancient synagogues. The various household and workshop vessels (1), charming mosaic pavement fragments (2) and smaller objects of daily life (3) from Beth-Shean are all typical of the Byzantine period throughout Israel.

In Crusader times (12th—13th centuries CE), lead *bullae* (4, Nos. 1 and 2) were used for sealing locks and strongboxes. One of these (No. 1) bears the seal of the Latin Patriarch of Jerusalem.

Crossing the room to cases (5) we see, amongst various glass, pottery and metal objects, several Coptic style ivory or bone carvings (at the right, on the wall panel). In case (6), note No. 1, a peculiar vessel ornamented in a "chip-carving" technique of the 6th—8th centuries CE.

Above: (2) Mosaic, Beth Shean, Byzantine period.
Below: (4) Seal of Latin patriarch of Jerusalem, 1158-1180 CE.

Islamic and Crusader Periods

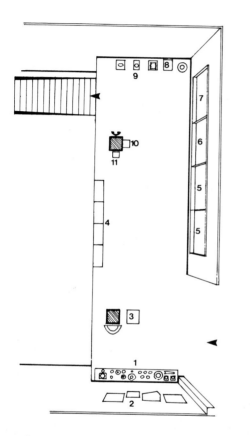

role under the aegis of the Umayyad capital at nearby Damascus. The importance of this period is reflected in the large number of finds at such Umayyad sites as Ramle. These include pottery made by many different techniques, among them molding, as can be seen in case (6, left). No. 3 is a mold for the neck of a jug, and is shown together with a modern impression made from it. This period was one of extensive monumental building projects and of widespread road construction, as fully revealed in the recent excavations in Jerusalem. Documentary evidence of this can be seen in the dedicatory inscription (11) of the Caliph Abd el-Malik.

Upon the succession of the Abbasid dynasty, attention shifted away from Israel and the country degenerated into a secondary province. The two-century Crusader episode left the ravaged land in the hands of the Ayubbids and, later, the Mamluks of Egypt, from whom it was wrested by the Ottoman Turks early in the 16th century. As part of the extensive Turkish empire, Israel was reduced even further, to the status of a district within a province, controlled from Damascus.

In case (7) on the right are various objects from a bath-house at Tiberias (12th century); note No. 2, the yellow glazed bowl with an incised bird pattern (12th-13th centuries); and No. 3, the very rare metal vessel with painted figures and Arabic script. On the left of the case is a pottery group from a shipwreck of the mid 18th century, discovered in the Gulf of Eilat.

The Crusader architectural fragments on display include an early 12th century capital (8) from the Church of the Annunciation in Nazareth, and mid 12th century stonework (9) from Kokhav Hayarden, the Crusader fortress of Belvoir which overlooks the Jordan river south of the Sea of Galilee.

Israel was under Muslim rule from 638 CE to 1917 — a period broken only by the Crusades in the 12th—13th centuries. Under such rule the Christians and Jews, although granted certain rights as privileged peoples, were reduced to secondary roles. The Umayyad period (661—750 CE) was the most important, for then, as in no subsequent period, the country enjoyed a central

In case (10), at the top of the stairway, is a splendid hoard of jewelry from the 10th—11th centuries, found at Caesarea. The filigree beads are some of the finest Islamic goldsmithing ever discovered in Israel.

Left: (10) Islamic gold jewelry, 10th-11th cents. CE.
Below: (8) Crusader capital, Castle Belvoir, 12th cent. CE.

Neighboring Cultures

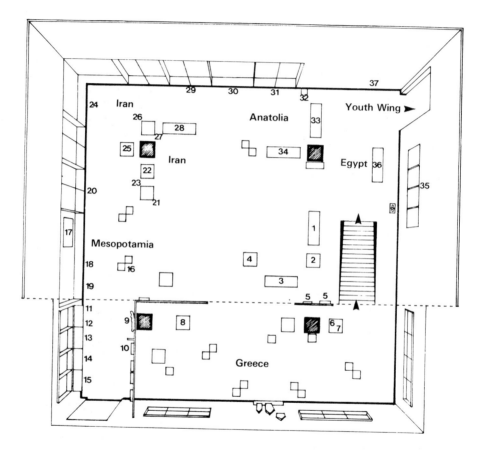

This gallery provides an insight into the ancient cultures of the countries surrounding Israel. All these lands are mentioned in the Bible, and several of them played prominent roles in the development of the Israelite nation.

Cyprus

Upon descending the staircase, and turning to the left, one encounters the display on Cyprus. This island, located in the midst of the principal Eastern Mediterranean cultures, was famous in antiquity for its pottery and metalwork. The rich copper deposits of Cyprus have long been exploited and this metal was exported as early as the third millennium BCE. The Cypriot Early Bronze Age (2050—1775 BCE) is represented by a variety of pottery from tombs (1). The Middle and Late Bronze Ages in Cyprus (18th—11th Centuries BCE) culminated in the rise of large urban centers. The Late Bronze Age is reflected here in figurines and a variety of pottery (2), of types exported throughout the Eastern Mediterranean basin, including Israel.

Cyprus was closely tied to the Mycenean culture of Greece and, upon the destruction of Mycenea at the end of the 13th century BCE, an influx of refugees stimulated Cypriot culture. Two centuries later another wave of migrants engulfed the island, apparently the Sea-Peoples, leading to the rise of the Cypro-Geometric culture (1050—700 BCE), represented by Cypro-Phoenician pottery (3) with its red burnish and black ornamentation. The chalice (4, No. 4 at the top), of the subsequent Cypro-Archaic culture (700—475 BCE), bears a heraldic bird motif reminiscent of Philistine pottery. Note also the naturalistic figure of a bird preening itself (4, No. 2).

The Greek World

On the panel behind case (3) is a small plaque (5, left) of the 7th century BCE, from Lydia in southwestern Anatolia; its gold filigree ornamentation depicts a winged goddess in a orientalized style. From the same region and period is the East Greek terracotta slab (5, right), with a painted depiction of a griffin and horseman. Stylistically, this piece is related to the Early Corinthian oinochoe (wine pitcher) of the late 7th century BCE (6), and to the adjacent pitcher (7).

The other pottery in this section — Classical Greek

(6) Early Corinthian oinochoe, 625-600 BCE.

painted vases, many of them bearing scenes from Greek mythology and daily life — is exemplified by a fine Attic "red-figured" amphora (8), apparently painted by Polygnotos, head of a school of vase-painters in Athens in the mid 5th century BCE. The scene shows the hero Theseus battling Amazons.

157

(12) Sumerian cylinder seal, ca. 3000 BCE.

Mesopotamia

Mesopotamia (modern Iraq) was the home of the early Sumerian culture, where writing was invented around 3,500—3,000 BCE. This earliest pictorial writing evolved into the cuneiform script, written upon tablets of clay (9) and on such early monuments as the rock relief from northeastern Iraq (9), showing a king of the early second millennium BCE, trampling his foe. Late in the third millennium BCE, the Sumerians were succeeded by the Akkadians, whose Semitic language now prevailed. An inscription engraved on a bronze bowl (10) mentions the conquests of Naram-Sin, the greatest king of Akkad.

Another significant Sumerian innovation was the cylinder seal, hallmark of Mesopotamian culture for several millennia. Cases (11-15) show the development of this interesting art of stone engraving. The agricultural basis of the Sumerian economy is seen in such motifs as a cow, a herd of cattle and ears of wheat (12). From around 2,800—2,400 BCE appear seals depicting mythological figures, especially a hero struggling with a beast (13), a recurring theme in Mesopotamian art and literature (14). The city of Babylon in central Mesopotamia rose to prominence in the 19th century BCE, ruled by Amorites of Semitic origin. Mainly religious scenes are found on the seals of this Old Babylonian period (15).

The bronze figurines (16) from the time of Gudea, ruler of Lagash, represents the Neo-Sumerian period.

The kingdom of Assyria rose in northern Mesopotamia toward the end of the second millennium BCE. King Ashurnasirpal II (883—859 BCE), who expanded this kingdom into an empire, is represented by a large relief (17) from a palace at ancient Calah (Nimrod); it depicts two winged figures flanking a sacred palm tree and performing a fertility rite. The inscription tells of the king's deeds. The small, adjacent relief (18), from the days of Ashurbanipal (668—631 BCE), depicts the head of a harnessed horse.

In Mesopotamia, a land lacking stone for construction, buildings were made of brick. The kings would often inscribe the bricks used in their royal projects (19): No. 4 bears the stamp of Sargon II, mentioned in the Bible as the conqueror of the northern kingdom of Israel; and No. 5 is of Nebuchadnezzar II, who destroyed Jerusalem in 586 BCE.

Iran

The vast land of Iran (Persia) lies in the uplands to the east of Mesopotamia. The large wall-case (20) outlines the development of Iranian pottery from the fifth millennium to the first millennium BCE. Some of the earlier painted pottery utilizes animal forms to obtain beautiful decorative patterns (note especially Nos. 4 and 5, from 3,500—3,000 BCE).

For thousands of years Iran was a center for the production of fine metalwork, as seen in the Sassanian silver of the 3rd—7th centuries CE (21). Adjacent case (22) contains objects from the period of the Parthians (250 BCE—226 CE), rivals of Rome in the east. Hellenistic style permeates these artifacts, especially the alabaster nude, the fine little bone statuette (Nos. 1 and 2), and the bronze vessel behind, in the corner, made in the form of a male god. The large silver plate (23), of the 6th—7th centuries CE, demonstrates the Sassanian tendency to abandon the Hellenistic style and return to oriental traditions.

The kingdom of Elam in Khuzistan, in southern Iran, arose early in history. Bordering southern Mesopotamia and having close ties with it, Elam is represented here by several 13th century BCE glazed tiles inscribed in cuneiform (24).

Case (25) displays various Sassanian gold jewelry; note No. 14 at the top, a cameo portrait of a king worked in lapis lazuli. The next case (26) and case (27) focus on Luristan in northwestern Iran, famous for its metalwork during the third to first millennia BCE. The importance attached to horse-breeding in this region is clearly seen, not only in the figurines themselves but also in the very nature of many of these objects — harness ornaments and bits.

(16) Neo-Sumerian copper figurine, ca. 2100 BCE.

159

Some of the most interesting Iranian pottery was made in the southern Caspian region (28), around the end of the second millennium BCE. The vessels often assumed animal forms, such as the humped bull (No. 3) and the graceful stag (No. 4).

Several waves of migration overwhelmed Iran from the north in antiquity. One of these, the Achemenid tribes coming out of Central Asia, led to the unification of all Iran, late in the 6th century BCE. The Achemenid empire, which ranged from Greece and Egypt in the west to India in the east, was founded by Cyrus the Great (550—530 BCE), who allowed the Jews to return to Jerusalem from Babylonian exile. The metal-work of Achemenid times, a high point in art by any standard, is represented here by the bronze, silver and gold vessels in case (29). This exquisite craftsmanship is matched in stone, in the lapis lazuli rhyton (No. 4). Clear evidence of Persian rule in Israel can be seen in the two bronze feet from a Persian style throne (on the right), found near Samaria. (Now in Persian Room, see page 130). The monumental splendor of this empire can be sensed in the fragments of basalt reliefs (30) from the stairway of the palace at Persepolis, the capital of Darius I (558—486 BCE).

Anatolia

Anatolia (modern Turkey) is a very diversified land in geography and climate, with equally varied peoples and cultures in antiquity. Case (31) reviews the pottery of this region, from the sixth millennium down to the second millennium BCE. As early as the sixth millennium BCE, southwestern Anatolia possessed an advanced culture which produced boldly fashioned pottery (31, right). Early in the third millennium BCE, in north-western Anatolia, the pottery and violin-shaped

(28) Stag-shaped vessel, Iran, early 1st mill. BCE.

160

ϵΡΓΟΝΑΛϵΞΑΝΛΡΟΥ

figurines (32) reveal considerable influence from the Aegean world. Later in the third millennium BCE, central Anatolia absorbed a wave of migrants who brought with them a new type of pottery, related to the contemporaneous Khirbet Kerak ware found in Israel (31, left, and see p. 100).

By the end of the third millennium BCE, Anatolian metalwork had reached a high standard. Some centuries later, written documents began revealing the rise of the Hittites, an Indo-European people mentioned in the Bible. The fine pottery of this period often reflects metal prototypes (31, left, Nos. 19-22). The Hittite empire soon rivalled Mesopotamia and Egypt. It was overthrown, however, in the 13th century BCE, probably by the Sea-Peoples — the same wave of warriors who overran the coast of Israel (see p. 113).

Early in the first millennium BCE, various smaller kingdoms rose throughout Anatolia, of which Phrygia in the central region and Lydia in the southwest were the most famous. The art of these two lands shows oriental and Greek influences (33).

In the Lake Van region of eastern Anatolia (Armenia), the minor empire of Urartu became a serious rival of the Assyrians in the 9th—7th centuries BCE. This was the Ararat of the Bible, and it was a land famous for its fine metalwork. Several of the bronze belts in case (34) are typical of the Urartian culture.

Egypt

The close relationship between Egypt and Israel in antiquity, from the Early Canaanite Age on, is clearly shown by the numerous objects of Egyptian art on display throughout the archaeological section of the museum. The modest display here is highlighted by

(33) Black burnished pottery jug, Anatolia 2000-1800 BCE.

(35) Egyptian relief, Amarna period, 14th cent. BCE.

several stone reliefs from the Amarna period (35), depicting blind musicians, harnessed horses, a face and the portrait of Akhenaton, the king who introduced a monotheistic cult into Egypt in the 14th century BCE. One of his successors was Tutankhamon.

Case (36) presents a selection of the many types of Egyptian amulets and scarabs; such objects are often found in excavations in Israel, and they greatly influenced local and Phoenician art, as can be seen in the carved ivories from Samaria (see p. 122).

Ruth Youth Wing

מהי אשליה?
what is illusion?

At this point one enters a very special world — the Ruth Rodman Frieman Youth Wing, planned and built for the specific needs of the younger visitors to the museum. The youth wing, which opened in 1966, moved to its present facilities in 1978 and is presently one of the largest and most active educational museum deparments of its kind in the world. It has its own galleries for temporary exhibitions (room 401, which you are now entering, and the gallery immediately downstairs), as well as classrooms, studios, workshops, a library, an auditorium and playgrounds.

The visitor — whether young or adult — is invited to roam through the wing and its facilities. The didactic exhibitions in the two galleries treat a diversity of subjects. Past themes have included the self-portrait, color and its uses, film-making, the childhood works of Israeli artists, embroidery, and many others. Extensive visitor participation is encouraged in these exhibitions, with materials provided for visitors to try their own hand at the current theme.

Special guided tours throughout the Israel Museum are provided by the youth wing for children during the school year, including workshop sessions on specific subjects. Lively contact is maintained with most of the schools in the Jerusalem region, supplementing the curriculum and introducing material not normally studied at school.

Art courses are held in a large variety of subjects: painting, drawing, sculpture, ceramics, woodwork, weaving, embroidery, photography, film-making, puppetry, drama, dance and pantomime. The children's annual courses are held in the afternoons (registration during August-September); the semi-annual adult courses (October-January and February-June terms) are held in the mornings and evenings. The youth wing's puppet theater gives performances in the auditorium, as well as appearances throughout the country (for other children's performances, see p. 169).

The Feinstein Library includes an extensive collection of children's illustrated books from various lands and the youth wing grants a biennial prize for the best Israeli illustrated children's book. Youth wing publications for teachers and children, providing supplementary material for schools and extra-curricular reading, are mostly in Hebrew (several have been translated into English and are obtainable from the youth wing or at the museum shop; see p. 169). A recycling project provides factory scraps and remnants for sale as creative materials for children, every Tuesday between 4 and 8 pm. The Archive of Reproductions and Travelling Exhibitions (see p. 168), is a department within the youth wing. The Paley Art Center for Youth adjoining the Rockefeller Museum in East Jerusalem, staffed and administered by the Ruth Youth Wing of the Israel Museum, commenced its activities in 1978 and serves both Arab and Jewish children with programs similar to those of the Ruth Youth Wing.

Archaeological Garden

Leaving the Youth Wing by its main entrance downstairs, one can turn to the right along the path to the Schenker Archaeological garden. The Roman copy of the Hellenistic "Woman" (1) was found at Ashkelon on Israel's coast. The two marble imitation vessels, opposite, are tomb-monuments of the 4th century BCE from Attica in Greece (2). The large marble statue of a Roman general in a heroic pose, on the far side of the garden, is of the 2nd century CE (3).

Turning up the steps to the left of the Roman general, we arrive back at the main gate and the exit from the museum grounds.

If you have checked anything at the *cloak-room* in the main building, don't forget to reclaim it.

Museum Services

The Israel Museum Library

Located in the Axel Springer Wing, the library contains 80,000 volumes and 230 periodicals on art and archaeology. The reading room serves the general public as well as the museum staff.

Reading hours: Sunday, Monday, Wednesday, Thursday, 10 am — 5 pm
Tuesday, 4 pm — 8 pm.

The Graphics Study Room

is reached by the circular staircase adjacent to room 212; it provides the public with the opportunity of studying the museum's collection of prints and drawings (see p. 48) at first hand. The student is able to examine the works of European, American and Israeli artists in the original. The study room includes a specialized reference library

Study hours: Sunday, Monday, Wednesday, Thursday, Friday, 11 am — 1 pm
Tuesday, 4 pm — 8 pm

The Archive of Reproductions and Travelling Exhibitions

located in the Ruth Youth Wing, has a collection of 300,000 reproductions and 30,000 photographic slides of works of art from all periods. It has prepared 250 travelling exhibitions covering a broad spectrum of art subjects. This material is utilized by schools, teachers' seminaries, kibbutzim, community centers and libraries throughout Israel. For a nominal fee these exhibitions are loaned out on a monthly basis, and the slides on a fortnightly basis.

Enquiries: 02-698211

Visiting hours: Sunday, Monday, Wednesday, Thursday, 8:30 am — 1 pm.
Tuesday, 3:30 pm — 6 pm

The Photographic Service

of the Israel Museum provides photographs, transparencies and slides (black-and-white or color) of objects from the museum collections. It serves individuals, researchers, publishers and other institutions on a commercial basis. (Many of the Israel Museum photographs are restricted to research use only.)

Enquiries: 02-698211, ext. 274

Office hours: Sunday — Friday, 9 am — 12 noon

The Excavations Department

The Israel Museum has engaged in archaeological fieldwork since 1965, mainly at Early Canaanite (Bronze Age) Arad in the Negev. At the museum itself, the department engages in the study of the finds from its excavations, mending and drawing the pottery, and comparative study. These activities enable the museum to enrich its collection and provide a means of study for scholars and students alike. Much of the department's work, especially in the field, is carried out by volunteers from Israel and abroad.

Enquiries concerning volunteer work in the department, including excavations: 02-698211, ext. 211.

Israel Museum Events

Tickets for the various events at the museum are available at the museum ticket office up to a week in advance or on the day of the event or performance. The bulletin board in the main lobby lists all current events, and information appears in notices in the press.

Israel Museum Film Club presents two performances every Tuesday, at 6 pm and 8:30 pm (auditorium).

Chamber Music Concerts are presented several times a month (auditorium).

Terrace Concerts are held during the summer (July-September) every Tuesday at 5 pm, on the Hermann Mayer Terrace for Performing Arts (entered through room 301, Prehistory).

Occasional performances of drama, dance and "performance art" are given, either in the auditorium or outdoors.

Lecture series are held regularly, often relating to current exhibitions.

Gallery talks are given on Tuesdays at 7:15 pm.

For Children: The museum presents films every Sunday, Monday, Wednesday and Thursday at 3:30 pm and, during the summer and holiday vacations, a matinée at 11 am.

Children's Concerts and theater performances are presented regularly, either in the auditorium or at the youth wing.

For further details, consult the bulletin board, the museum's monthly bulletin or notices in the press.

Museum Shop

The museum shops are located in the main entrance and the entrance hall of the museum building, with an annex in the Shrine of the Book. The shops are closed on Saturdays and holidays. The shops have a wide selection of gifts, museum replicas (archaeology, Judaica, modern art), postcards and posters, jewelry, books on art, archaeology, Israel and Jerusalem — in English, German, French, Spanish and Hebrew — and children's books and games.

Orders are accepted by mail (address: The Museum Shop, The Israel Museum, Hakirya, Jerusalem 91012, Israel). A pro forma invoice will be sent and, upon receipt of payment, the order will be dispatched by air or surface mail, as specified.

Friends of the Israel Museum

Friends of the Israel Museum has 7,000 members in Israel. Friends participate in special activities, receive the monthly museum bulletin and enjoy reductions at the museum shop and at museum events. The membership card also grants free entrance to the Rockefeller Museum in Jerusalem, the Tel Aviv Museum and Museum Ha'aretz in Tel Aviv and the Haifa Museum. "Shoharim" (local patrons) are invited to all exhibition openings and special events.

For details of annual membership fees apply to the museum ticket office, the information desk or the museum offices, 02-698211, ext. 214 or 255.

The International Organization of Patrons has some 350 members, patrons and guardians who receive the museum's catalogues and are invited to attend the annual international council meeting. The list of patrons and guardians of the Israel Museum is published annually in the *Museum News*.

Hakirya, Jerusalem 91012, tel. 02-698211 ext. 290.

Friends of the Israel Museum Abroad

The following organizations are associated with the Israel Museum and channel contributions and gifts from abroad.

The American Friends of the Israel Museum, 10 East 40th Street, New York, N.Y. 10016, tel. 212-683-5190 (recognized charity for tax benefits in U.S.)

The Canadian Committee of Friends of the Israel Museum, Suite 700, 2 St. Clair Avenue East, Toronto, Ontario M4T 2T5, (recognized charity for tax benefits in Canada)

Robert Indiana's Sculpture 'Ahava' during multi-media show

The British Friends of the Art Museums of Israel, 1 Rodmarton Street, London W1H 3FW, tel. 01-486-3954 (gifts, legacies and bequests are substantially free of Capital Transfer Tax in U.K.)

Les Amis du Musée d'Israël en France, 256 rue Marcadet, Paris 75018, tel. 01-229-2597

For further information contact:
The Department for Public Affairs, The Israel Museum, Hakirya, Jerusalem 91012, tel. 02-698211 ext. 290.

Donors of exhibits illustrated in the Museum Guide

Many of the objects and works of art reproduced have been presented by friends of the Museum. Most gifts made in the United States were presented through the America-Israel Cultural Foundation up to 1972, and after that date to the American Friends of the Israel Museum.

Unless otherwise stated, archaeological objects are lent and published by kind permission of the Israel Department of Antiquities and Museums.

COLOR PLATES: